NINA HERE

NOR THERE

My Journey Beyond Gender

NICK KRIEGER

Beacon Press
Boston

Beacon Press
25 Beacon Street
Boston, Massachusetts 02108-2892
www.beacon.org

Beacon Press books
are published under the auspices of
the Unitarian Universalist Association of Congregations.

14 13 12 11   8 7 6 5 4 3 2 1

Text design by Yvonne Tsang
at Wilsted & Taylor Publishing Services

Library of Congress Cataloging-in-Publication Data
Krieger, Nick.
Nina here nor there : my journey beyond gender /
Nick Krieger.
p. cm.
ISBN 978-0-8070-0092-2 (pbk. : alk. paper)
1. Krieger, Nick, 1978– 2. Transsexuals—California—
San Francisco—Biography. 3. Sexual minorities—
California—San Francisco. I. Title.
HQ77.8.K75A3 2011
306.76'8092—dc22 [B]   2010050226

This is a true story. However, the names and
other identifying details of some of the persons
(and one cat) have been changed to protect privacy.

For
The Boys

CONTENTS

One

TA-TA TATAS

On a Saturday afternoon in May, tucked into a friend's backyard near my house in San Francisco's Castro neighborhood, only a few blocks from the supersize rainbow flag, the memorial triangle of pink stones, and the landmark marquee of the Castro Theatre, women surrounded me. They were my older, established, financially secure, coupled-off, home-buying, capital-*L* Lesbian—as in women-loving-women—friends. With money, influence, and good looks, they weren't quite mainstream, but part of the emerging gaystream, those targeted by the *New York Times,* Hillary Rodham Clinton, and marketers of the pantsuit. I called them my A-gays.

Our host, Stephanie, appeared at the top of the stairs, sporting a J. Crew sweater, gold necklace, and designer jeans that hid a small tattoo by her hip. "Helloooo, ladies!" she shouted, before descending into the yard. Her girlfriend, Beth, followed close behind, sporting a collared shirt, silver thumb ring, and cheap khakis that hid a small tattoo by her ankle.

After a lifetime in the women's athletic scene, I was accustomed to the understated casual wear, parties reminiscent of half-time huddles, and a definition of "ladies" that implied ass kicking rather than good manners. My connection to everyone in the backyard crew stemmed from soccer, a sport I'd stopped playing a couple years before, tired of competition and commitments that required me to run around at specific times.

I came to this postgame gathering to see Zippy, a tiny and witty monkey-like thing who'd recently moved to LA for a film career and was back in town for a visit. She and I were younger than the others, less accomplished, A-gays in training—although we weren't really on course to pass the entrance exam. We sat across from each other on folding camping chairs, rickety on the yard's uneven slabs of stone. Pockets of flowerbeds and banks of shrubbery sprouted around us, the dirt still wet from the morning rain.

"Well, isn't this my lucky day," Stephanie said, placing one hand on my shoulder and the other on Zippy's. "A special day indeed when you kids come out to join us."

Zippy sprang out of her seat, shooting her tricolor pompadour-mullet to the sky. "Well, wouldn't you know, it's my lucky day too, be-otch."

The two of them hugged before Stephanie opened her arms toward me. "Always a pleasure."

Had Stephanie not meant every word, her exaggerated pleasantries would've been embarrassing. I felt myself blush all the same from her kindness.

"How's your writing?" she asked.

"Yeah, how is your writing?" Beth seconded. "And when do I get to see what you've been working on?" She winked, just as she did at the office when she caught me with one of my essays open on my computer.

Beth had contracted me to do web writing at the bank where she worked and considered my employment "supporting the arts," as did a handful of other A-gays I'd worked odd jobs for over the past three years. They couldn't get enough of the mass e-mails and blog posts I sent from my trips—backpacking in Eastern Europe and Southeast Asia, bicycling from Canada to Mexico— and, much to my appreciation, always helped my traveling-writer lifestyle by employing me and buying me drinks whenever I was back in San Francisco.

I knocked around a few pebbles with the toe of my hiking boot. "At the rate I'm going, I'll have some quality writing in a few years," I said.

"And I got first dibs," Zippy jumped in.

"Well, I'll be waiting patiently." Beth offered me an encouraging smile before turning to Zippy. "For your next film project as well."

Zippy motioned me back down to our seats and scooted hers closer. "So, what *are* you working on?" she whispered.

Ever since Zippy had read one of my early travelogues, forwarded by a mutual friend, she'd been my biggest fan. When I returned from that trip, she found my number and called me six times in one day, begging to hang out, a near stalking that might've scared me had I not been laughing so hard from her messages. We ended up chatting for hours about our book and film influences and passions, barely stopping to breathe. For a few weeks, early in our friendship, I thought I might be in love with her, until the moment she flipped upside down on her couch, inhaled a whip-it balloon, and I knew she was too out of control to date. Zippy was a best pal, the only one I'd ever showered with, which had happened once when we were unable to pause an exciting conversation.

Of all the things I'd missed about Zippy since she moved, it was our artistic talks, creative speed as we called it, that I missed the most. I told her about the essay collection I was developing out of an unfinished one-woman show she and I had collaborated on about my futile quest to find a girlfriend, now going on nearly seven years.

"Who's your latest crush, or should I say character?" Zippy gibed, nudging my foot with hers as if we were both in on the joke that my life only existed to serve my writing. "Let me guess, unrequited?"

"Yeah. She's straight." I avoided Zippy's eyes, knowing they would be both chiding and compassionate, as I described the flighty girl in my graduate writing program. "She confessed to having a crush on me. Then for the next three months, whenever we went to a bar after class, she made sure she was never left alone with me."

"Classic." Zippy slapped her leg a few times. A half-dozen zippers fluttered on her baggy pants. They looked like something Michael Jackson would've designed for MC Hammer, but on Zippy they seemed cool. Everything did.

From my jeans, I pulled out a glass bowl and weed from a medical dispensary. I'd claimed "anxiety" to receive my cannabis card, although "New York City Jew" would've been equally accurate. I packed the bowl and waited for Zippy to take the first hit.

"It gets worse," I said. I lit the last patch of green and inhaled deeply. "I finally got her alone and made a move. She said she wasn't ready." I blew out my frustration in a huge cloud of smoke. "The following week, she asked me to walk her home *and* invited me up. We ended up messing around in her bed. I stayed over, but no sex. She said she wanted to, but pulled 'time of the month.' I still don't believe her." I tapped the pipe against my hand. The ashy residue stuck. "We met up a few days later at a literary event. She brought some guy. He groped her the whole time."

"Why do you do this to yourself?" Zippy asked.

"Dude, this guy was such a loser. She could do so much better."

"Like you?"

"Yes, like me."

"But she's not a lesbian."

I banged the pipe on the stone at my feet, nearly cracking it. In the hammock across the yard, two women lay entwined, swinging gently. Next to them, Beth was curled into Stephanie's lap. "I prefer straight girls," I said.

"You do see the problem, right? They don't like the hooha."

I grabbed my Milwaukee's Best, one of the many leftover cans from the soccer field, out of the chair's cup holder. The beer tasted like piss, but I chugged the rest, the same move I made when anyone implied they might want to get near my hooha. Leaning back into my chair, I could see through the protective cover of the trees. My eyes followed the white trail of clouds off into the distance. "I could really use a trip," I said.

"It hasn't even been a year. Aren't you just getting settled?" Zippy said. "How are your new digs, anyway?"

I thought of the parties at my house, my roommates' friends with tattoo sleeves and septum piercings, boyish and manly dykes flaunting all that had been ingrained in me as disreputable. "It's an education." Picturing the chest scars of the few folks who often went topless on my back deck, I added, "And then some."

I pulled a flier out of my jeans pocket, one of the many left lying around my kitchen. I unfolded it to reveal a grayscale guillotine, designed not with one hole for a head, but two holes. For breasts.

"Whoa," Zippy said.

I felt relieved to see her large blue eyes expand as she stared at the words *Ta-Ta Tatas* on the top of the flier. My roommates talked about their friend Greg's top-surgery fund-raiser as if it was a common occurrence, like raising money for the AIDS ride as some of the A-gays did annually. I glanced at the flier again, at the guillotine. It was both sacrilegious and curious.

"I think I saw this on MySpace. You wanna go? There'll be hot girls there." Zippy sang the last word like an enticing advertising jingle.

I anxiously patted my jeans for the pipe. "Do you even know Greg?"

"Not well. Just from flag football. I found out about her— I mean his—transition from our teammates." I'd forgotten Zippy had played flag football with Greg and many of the others who hung around my new house. With a history of outsider experiences only a few people knew about, Zippy was deeply empathetic. Her greatest skill, other than a left-footed soccer cross, was chatting up the visitor from out of town, the wallflower, the lone guy, or the solo guest at a party to make them feel included. "I'd like to support him," she said.

"I want to support him, too." I jostled my legs, feeling the start of pins and needles where the backs of my thighs molded to my seat. "Although I'm not entirely sure why."

"If Greg thinks he'll be happier as a guy, then he should go for it."

"It can't be that simple." I stood up, shook out my legs and un-wrapped my hoodie from my waist. "What does that even mean?"

As I zipped up my sweatshirt, Stephanie walked over. "You're not leaving, are you?"

The sun dipped behind the hill. I pulled the hood over my head and dug my hands into my pockets. "Just cold."

"We're going to Greg's benefit party," Zippy said as if I'd already agreed. "Wanna come?"

"Do I know Greg?" Stephanie asked.

"He plays flag football," Zippy said. "He used to be Kerry. He's having a fund-raiser for top surgery."

Stephanie looked at Zippy and then back to me. I felt uneasy, as if an unmarked dividing line between two social circles was cracking under my feet.

Stephanie crossed her arms, pushing a bit of cleavage into the V-neck of her black sweater. "I'll leave this one to you kids," she said, patting us both on the shoulder. "But if you want to stick around and get cozy, I'm about to get this fire started."

I watched Stephanie head back across the patio and enlist Beth's help in carrying the stand-alone pit from the corner of the backyard, springing everyone into action. Someone grabbed the pile of wood left over from the last bonfire, and another went inside for newspaper. They would be there all night; they always were, their gatherings like the San Francisco monoseason—sixty degrees and partly cloudy with a chance of wind and fog—com-fortable and easy, so predictable and unchanging as to be suffo-cating.

"I wanna go," I said to Zippy. "Let's go."

"Now you're clucking, big chicken." She popped a set of car keys out of a canvas shoulder bag and dangled them in front of my eyes. "I'll even drive."

We said good-bye to a few of the A-gays and said we'd be back, a statement Zippy believed but I did not. When she turned on the car, the stereo blasted a female vocalist. She turned the volume down, barely, aware of my preference for conversation over ear damage, and started to tell me how her long-distance girlfriend, Sonia, thought transgender people were setting back the progress of gays and lesbians.

I listened to her ramble about the inequality of civil unions and "Don't Ask, Don't Tell" while I stared outside the window as the streetscape changed from colorful Victorian houses to high-end restaurants, taquerias, and convenience stores displaying Spanish-language ads for money-wire services.

"I don't have a stake in marriage and the military," I conceded, turning the knob on the radio volume down further to avoid having to yell. "But I still don't understand the 'my turn first, your turn later' mentality."

"Hey, me neither," Zippy assured me. "Sonia just doesn't know any transgender people in East Bumblefuck. It's still scary to her. So, I told her about SF peeps and set her straight. But not too straight." Zippy hit the gas and flipped the volume up to full blast. Belting the chorus, she cruised the last few blocks and pulled headfirst into a metered spot. We parked close enough to the neighborhood dive that I could see a bunch of people smoking and talking on cell phones by the entrance. From the outside, the crowded scene didn't seem all that different from that at the monthly dyke party I used to attend regularly there.

At the door, a woman leaned over a cash box collecting donations, her T-shirt emblazoned with the image of the breast guillotine. I turned to the place in my brain that craves reason, but it fell silent as I handed over my twenty dollars.

The bar was packed, the drink line two deep. It took nearly ten minutes to order a Dos Equis for me and a rum and Diet Coke for Zippy. With the drinks in my hands, I followed her past the pool table and outside onto the deck, where C+C Music Factory blasted through the speakers. Two DJs, well-known names in the party circuit, leaned over turntables on one side of the courtyard.

Surveying the scene, I spotted my roommate Jess making

out with the barista from a local coffee shop across the threshold of what appeared to be a lemonade stand with the words *Kiss me baby!* painted on the booth. The barista wore only a black bra, and from the length of the kiss, I doubted any money had been exchanged. My other roommate Melissa, one of the many wearing the breast guillotine T-shirt, milled through the crowd. Wearing her faded red jeans, and with her sunglasses perched on top of her curly hair, she looked like a field hockey coach swallowed by a rock concert.

Down in the dance pit, hundreds of feet slammed against the concrete. Heads bopped and swayed. Arms and hands reached up toward the darkening sky. A festoon of dingy, colored lightbulbs ran across a stage packed with partygoers doing the bump 'n' grind. Everywhere I looked people were making out, trading partners left and right and left again, like an orgiastic square dance.

I hightailed it to the far end of the promenade as if I might catch the bacchanalian cooties. These were the people who had reclaimed all the slurs; who welcomed fetishes and BDSM*; who dubbed themselves sex-positive, fought for the rights of sex workers, and honored stripping and porn—as long as it was women owned and run. They had long since chucked the shackles of normalcy into the Bay, where some of them probably frolicked naked, covered in glitter, or as one girl did now with only pasties over her nipples. They even thought being called queer, with its connotation of weird and radical, was a compliment.

"I can't handle this party," I yelled to Zippy, and sipped my beer. I instantly regretted not ordering two. "This is chaos."

I missed my A-gays, my coupled-off monogamous friends who cried "helloooo, ladies," my friends who wouldn't dare hit the beach without their most flattering bikinis, their bodies waxed and shaved, my friends who had been to Palm Springs for the Dinah Shore lesbian weekend of the year at least once, my friends who

---

*Bondage and discipline, dominance and submission, sadism and masochism.

were all unmistakably women. With my jeans and low-rise hiking boots, my plain low-key style, at least I blended in with them. At least we collectively blended in with the rest of society.

"I promise we won't stay long," Zippy shouted back. "Come on." She wrapped her tiny fingers around my hand and tugged me a few steps closer to the festivities.

Greg lumbered over to us, his gait heavy with big guy swagger and accented by a metal chain that connected his keys to saggy jeans. He wore the now-familiar breast guillotine T-shirt and a black Kangol newsboy cap, cocked sideways over strands of unkempt hair that hung down by his pierced ears. With his stony eyes, hard-set jaw, and stance that often boxed me out of conversations, his cold attitude intimidated me.

A couple of months ago, right after I learned about his new name, Greg was over at my house, grilling steaks with Jess. Heading out from my bedroom to microwave my own dinner, I found Greg in my kitchen doorway talking into his cell phone, his back and stocky frame blocking my way. I tried to get his attention with "excuse me," and only when he didn't budge did I contemplate using "Greg." But he hadn't even told me about his new name himself. I'd simply listened as my roommates used "Greg" excessively in conversation, breaking it in like a newly oiled baseball glove, slapping the ball against the leather. I feared his name hadn't solidified enough for him to recognize it instantly, or that he might scream, "You don't know me. Who are you to call me Greg?" So much was captured in that name, in the fact that he had changed it, and I hadn't yet formally met the guy in my kitchen. "Excuse me, Greg," I finally said, and he moved aside without hesitation.

Zippy ran up to Greg and I slipped behind her to trail. "Hello, Greg!" she screamed.

"Thank you so much for coming." He hugged Zippy and then me, an embrace that was more bear hug than formality.

Zippy bounced in place to the music. "This is a great fucking party."

"You have no idea how relieved I am." Greg readjusted his cap and sighed. In his exhale, I sensed the desperation behind his well-executed fund-raiser. He broke into a warm smile, his toughness disappearing like a mirage. It would still be a while before I noticed that those were not hawks tattooed on his forearms, but doves. "Congratulations, Greg," I eked out as he dashed off to a group of his trans friends.

I watched him exchange a high five with someone I'd met at one of my roommates' flag football parties once. A shirt dangled like a rag from his jeans; his exposed chest was smooth and flat. With chest scars and a slightly pear-shaped body, he looked half-male, half-female, and I found myself feeling sorry for him. He pulled his shirt from his jeans and whirled it around his head like a lasso, a huge smile on his face. Seeing his uninhibited happiness, my pity turned into annoyance.

Zippy had a shit-eating grin on her face, her body lost in the rhythm of an '80s tune. Shifting my weight from one foot to the other, I tried to let the beat flow into me. I ordered my shoulders into action and immediately felt my own awkwardness, imagined everyone else could see it as well. My legs stiffened and my entire body went hard, like clay in a kiln. "I'm not feeling this party," I said. "If you want to stay, that's cool."

Zippy pointed to an old fling going at it with someone neither of us deemed attractive and swore she'd never sleep with her again. She got my mind off my own self-consciousness by engaging me in a game where we took turns pointing out bad decision couplings. It worked for a while, until I realized everyone had someone to make out with—everyone but me.

The leaves of a lush tree spilled over the high-rise concrete wall into the courtyard, reminding me of the rain forests in Costa Rica, my hiking and zip-line adventures through the jungle. I started to plan a savings schedule and travel budget in my head, adding and subtracting numbers, calming myself with the math of escape the way someone else might repeat a mantra.

In the dance pit, I saw a woman I'd once written a poem about kiss someone who wasn't cute. I turned to Zippy. "Really, I want to go," I repeated.

"I'll be ready to leave soon. Just give me one more round." Zippy rubbed her hands together and placed them on my head, smoothing my short brown hair down into a side part. "You just stay here and look pretty. I'll be back in two shakes."

After Zippy left, I moved deeper into the corner of the deck and situated myself on the railing to wait. On the far side of the courtyard, I saw one of my neighbors, someone who'd once dated a friend of mine back before his transition. When I first met him he looked like your average woman, even had shoulder-length curly hair. I remembered him as all bones and clumsiness in his female body. Now he'd filled out, grown solid, hardened. I often saw him tramp down our street, his head high, chest out, like a proud rooster. It was as if I'd witnessed a demon expelled, a body once possessed with an ungainly lack of control relieved of a ghost.

Lately, it seemed like these trans guys, as most people referred to them, were everywhere—bars, bookstores, parks, my house, my street—their very presence refuting what I'd always taken as fact, that those with an *F* on their birth certificates were automatically women. Before moving to the Castro, I'd thought becoming a man was as realistic as growing wings. Asking whether a woman would be happier as a guy was one of those dumb questions, like what would you do if a genie emerged from a bottle and granted you three wishes, or what super power would you most like to have.

Watching from the raised platform of the deck, above a sea of beanies and baseball caps, camouflage and corduroy, red mohawks and bleached faux hawks, track jackets and hoodies, argyle cardigans and soccer jerseys, I wondered what the fundamental difference was between me and the rest of the guests at the party, between me and Greg. I knew I wasn't the only one mistaken for a boy in the women's restroom every couple of weeks. The correction came quickly, after a second glance at my chest or face. I didn't care much one way or the other; the "wrong bathroom" thing happened to everyone who looked like me.

Before top surgery and testosterone had broken on to the social scene, I wouldn't have noticed the distinctions between me and Greg beyond our choices in fashion. But all of a sudden, or so it seemed, many people I saw as dykes were pursuing physical alterations, highlighting differences that had been previously invisible to the naked eye.

In this environment, it was impossible for me to tell what gender cues—things like earrings, hairstyle, underwear preference, and body hair—meant to a person, whether someone with leg hair thought of herself as a free-spirited womyn or himself as a virile man. The style signposts had once held masculine or feminine connotations that helped me define a person, but here they failed to indicate whether a person self-identified as man, woman, or something else entirely. I figured earrings and longish hair would be the first things someone like Greg would lose, small changes to prevent being perceived as a woman. But then again, plenty of dudes wore earrings and overgrown hair, too.

Greg hopped in place near the stage, intermittently hugging folks on their way out. At the end of the song, the emcee, a towering woman in drag queen regalia, stepped up to the platform. "Say good-bye to Greg's tatas," she shouted, trilling the last word in operatic fashion before handing Greg the mike. Holding it close to his mouth in hip-hop style, he thanked everyone for their support, calling out my roommates by name.

His white T-shirt shined bright under the string of dim lights. If I hadn't seen the gigantic breast guillotine on the front, if I hadn't been at his top-surgery fund-raiser, if I hadn't known that he had consciously changed his name to Greg, I would've thought he was just another dyke, more butch than me, but a dyke all the same. How did he know he wasn't? And when had he first known? He had to be in his early thirties, at least—not much older than me. I took the last swig of my beer, clanked it into a nearby plastic bin, and jumped off the railing.

On my way inside, I spotted Zippy in the DJ area with a headphone to her ear, flipping through a milk crate of records. Since the bathroom line was shorter than the bar line, I got behind a handful of people waiting for the women's single stall.

"What's behind the other door?" someone a few paces up asked.

"There's a urinal," a different voice replied. "And no lock on the door."

"I pissed all over myself the last time I tried to use it," said the woman in front of me. "I'm bald as an eagle down there." She spread her legs and locked her knees. "Dribbled straight down my leg."

"I peed all over my shoes. I don't get how girls do it."

I tried to refrain from chuckling. Every time I stood in this line it was the same conversation, and the urinal wasn't that hard to use.

A newcomer approached the line, scanned the trail out to the courtyard, and asked if anyone wanted to cover her. Everyone in front of me looked around blankly. I stepped out of the line and guarded the door after she entered. A few minutes later, we traded spots.

Inside the bathroom, the tiled floor was sticky and the stench of pee overpowering. I dropped my jeans and boxers, straddled the base of the urinal rising from the ground, and bent my knees slightly, keeping my butt a few centimeters from the porcelain. The stream pounded the drain with the backsplash hitting the floor and my hiking boots. With no toilet paper around, I gave up the idea of wiping, instead air-drying and zipping up. The soap dispenser had been ripped off the wall. Typical, I thought. All this place needed was some porn mags to be the quintessential men's room. I rinsed my hands, not caring about soap, TP, piss on my shoes, or which bathroom I chose.

Zippy spotted me coming out of the bathroom and slipped inside before the door shut behind me. She bragged about her ability to pee anywhere and had once done so into a Ziploc bag while stuck in a car during a traffic jam. It's how she got her name, although I imagine it held because she zipped around at warp speeds.

While waiting, I caught my roommate Melissa walking down the corridor. Compared to the other guests at the party, she came across as ordinary, a garden-variety lesbian more like my A-gays or me. "Having a good time?" I asked.

"I'm having a blast. Best party of my life." Her ruddy face, nearly as bright as her red pants, beamed with joy. "Greg's raised like $5,000."

She told me about the raffles, the kissing booth, the money pouring in from all directions, especially the date auction. There had been a bidding war for one pair. "It's too bad you missed it. It was crazy—Justine dropped $720! I've never seen anything like it."

It was a shit ton of money, and I figured that even with his store clerking wage, Greg could save the rest. "You helped make it happen," I congratulated Melissa. Utilizing her nonprofit fund-raising skills, she'd been a major orchestrator of the party planning.

"Do you know how many families you could feed for $5,000?" Melissa lifted her empty beer to her lips and tipped it back to no avail. "But as long as Greg's happy." She inspected the green glass bottle and shrugged. "I think I need more beer." She disappeared into a bar crowd that didn't appear to be letting up.

On the way out, I told Zippy about all the money Greg had raised, Justine's donation in particular. "Can you imagine?" I asked. "Giving someone $720 to lop off their breasts?"

"How much does it cost?" Zippy asked.

"About eight grand."

"Damn, dog." Zippy led us out of the bar without looking back. "I'm glad we chipped in."

Twenty bucks wasn't much, but I was proud to offer something. I admired Greg for putting himself out there and being public with his need. It wasn't until I spoke to Justine a couple of months later, asked her why she donated such a large sum, that I would fully comprehend the size of her contribution and the larger cause. She would tell me that the bidding war itself was a fix, set up by her and her friends, and that the money came from her graduate student loans, doled out to her at the beginning of each semester in huge portions that she would have to pay back. She would also say that every person who feels more comfortable in the queer community is an example, a person to look up to to make society more accepting.

I followed Zippy outside, closed the bottom half of the stable door behind me, and stepped onto the quiet sidewalk. The sky held no trace of the early rain or clouds, and stretched off toward the horizon clear and expansive. Without thinking, I reached up and absentmindedly fiddled with an earring. I slid out first one, then the other, sticking the silver hoops deep into the recesses of my pocket.

Two

HOME

About a year before Ta-Ta Tatas, I'd come back to San Francisco from my latest travel stint—a winter spent snowboard bumming with my brother in Jackson Hole, Wyoming. Upon my return, I couch-surfed and subletted for a couple months until a friend told me about the available room in the Castro house, and I checked it out immediately. The bedroom had a brick fireplace and bay windows, the house had a washer/dryer and a huge private back deck, and the neighborhood was safe enough that even with my native New Yorker paranoia, I wouldn't hit the deck when cars backfired.

When I discovered the incredibly low rent, I felt as if I'd won the urban living lottery. Not only had my prospective new housemates assured me that their dirty dishes skipped three-day pit stops in the sink, but they were acquaintances, and with that came the familiarity of having seen each other around for a few years. After we all agreed I'd be a good addition to the house, I went over to sign the lease. Only Jess was around, stuck engaging with me and my excessive deliberations that accompanied big decisions.

Sitting in low-lying picnic chairs on the back deck, Coronas on the Astroturf by our feet, I fired away redundant questions about bills, noise, cleanliness, and guests. With her youthful face, lady-killer smile, and smooth strut, Jess had reminded me, in our passings from afar, of a star Little League shortstop. Now that we were deep in conversation, there was something about her even temperament and composure, her fair skin and the subtle yet distinguished arch of her nose, that brought to mind a polished marble statue. As she calmly waited for me to run out of ways to rephrase myself, the clouds above us raced across the sky, the fog rolling in from Twin Peaks as if snowballing down the hill. "You know, I've never lived with all dykes before," I finally said.

After a winter of small ski-town life, no homos to be found—and I did the due diligence of asking around—my return to the gay mecca had caused me some culture shock. I feared that living all dyke all the time could be isolating, make it hard to remain in greater society, be part of company events, bachelorette parties, and golf vacations with my family.

Jess rolled down the sleeves of her white Hanes T-shirt. "Don't you want to live with your community, with other queers."

When I thought about it, my golf clubs had gathered mouse poop in storage, I'd never been invited to a bachelorette party, and the last time I'd worked for a company that threw corporate parties was during the dot-com era. Jess also seemed to be stating a fact rather than asking a question, and I knew then that she was persuasive. What I didn't know was that soon we'd be using each other to test ourselves in countless discussions that would inform who we were and who we would become. I also didn't know the slight distinction between lesbians and queers when I cashed in my lottery ticket.

At parties at my new house, these queers invaded my back deck, living room, and kitchen. With their mural-size tattoos, chin piercings, outfits that belonged in music videos, and distinguishing transgender marks like chest scars and pubescent facial hair, they blared a standoffish attitude, apathetic and indifferent to everyone who might be glaring. And everyone was. Flashing like neon signs that read, "I don't give a fuck about normal," they were not fit dinner company for parents—or at least not mine on the East Coast, who needed to know SAT scores, intentions of MBA, MD, or JD, and golf handicap before the shrimp cocktail arrived. I was impressed and intimidated by the confidence it took to stand out, but I couldn't help feeling a little personally offended, as if our houseguests were also flipping me off for trying to exist quietly and assimilate into the gaystream.

Melissa was the first of my new housemates and their crew to put me at ease. She was an outsider like her friends, although her otherness seemed to stem not from gender, sexuality, or her body, but from her roots. Raised north of the border, Melissa had the Canadian sensibility, a carefree cheerfulness unseen in the States, as if being isolated for months under a ton of snow made a person shrug and say, "What are you going to do, eh?" and pull out a beer. I'd discovered my love for Canadians during my travels, a time when I'd also learned to enjoy being an outsider myself, as the only American in certain hostels and towns.

Melissa's presence grounded me as my eyes adjusted to our regular guests practicing bondage knots, reading passages from *The Ethical Slut* (aka the bible of polyamory), and playing games that involved shots, whipped cream, and wrestling. Even when intoxicated, I tried to avoid social activities that required me to touch, let alone eat food out of another human being's belly button. Mostly, I hung on the sidelines, in the corners, and blended into the wallpaper.

I found myself paying special attention to the trans guys. Through observation and eavesdropping, I developed a vague understanding of the terms *transgender, testosterone,* and *top surgery*—the last my focus from the first moment I noticed Bec. It was at one of our house parties, a few months after I moved in, that my fascination with her began. Pushing six feet with broad shoulders, she stood out like a lone skyscraper among the rest of the flag football players, commanding center stage with her physical presence alone. She held it with her charisma and strong, mellifluous voice, rallying the others in a one-on-one flag-grabbing competition for which she played both referee and ringleader, springing gracefully around my back deck wearing only a pair of long athletic shorts.

From my spot on the side of the stairs, I honed in on Bec's chest, focused on the white lines visible there, faint symmetrical scars that ran from her armpits to sternum. In one moment they loomed as large as saber wounds, and in the next, as miniscule as paper cuts. I stared at those dull lines, bored in, piercing them as if trying to break the skin, the rib cage, and lock on to the heart. Why did you do this, I wondered. When does a woman interrupt the daily routine of living to decide to have a mastectomy, before morning coffee or after the mail arrives? Why would Rebecca remove her breasts but keep her female name?

Bec was confusing—beautiful and handsome, amorphous and alluring, a stallion or a mare, I had no idea. So I watched her, always, as did everyone else. A consummate performer, Bec danced, sang, lip-synched, and strip-teased, treating life as if it were a musical rated NC-17. Bec could've played any role made for an adolescent boy, slipping easily into high school quarterback or down-and-out hustler, but '50s greaser Danny Zuko came most naturally. In front of my large living room mirror, she'd often run her palms along the greased sides of her neatly combed hair, and then with her right hand she'd stroke her tight white T-shirt diagonally from the shoulder, running her hand over her chest as if still enamored by its flatness. Whenever possible, Bec did not wear a shirt.

That was how I found Bec, topless, in my kitchen on a Sunday morning a week after Greg's fund-raiser. Technically, Bec dated my third roommate, Erin. In actuality, Bec was more like my third roommate. She had a key to the house long before Erin moved in, and would keep it long after Erin moved out.

Bec was cracking eggs over a glass bowl, the cuffs of her blue jeans rolled above her bare feet, the waist hanging low on her narrow hips. By now, I was used to Bec shirtless, intimate with the intricacies of the enormous mosaic tattoo on her back. Turning toward the stove, Bec jumped when she saw me. I was always doing that, scaring people, a lurker in my own home.

"Good morning, Nina," she said upon recovery, sounding pleasant as ever.

Coming from Bec, my name rang like chimes, melodious and

pretty. My jaw hardened and I offered a solid nod. "Morning," I said. I noticed her faded chest scars fleetingly, as I still always did upon first glance, with a brief thought about what was there once and was no longer.

"You're welcome to join us. There's more than enough bacon to go around." Bec looked like she needed all the protein she could get. With her reedy body and smooth hairless chest, she seemed forever on the cusp of male puberty.

"Thanks, but I don't really eat meat," I said. "And I'm kind of addicted to cereal."

Bec disappeared into the other room. I grabbed the three boxes of cereal I wanted to mix and pulled my soymilk out of the refrigerator. When I saw Bec's new addition to our fridge photo gallery, I froze. There were already two high school photos up, one of Melissa in bright red lipstick and a Victorian costume dress, the other a senior class photo of her friend Monster—hair permed and lip gloss, blush, and eye makeup applied with a butter knife—both ironic nods to the past, a photographic graveyard of girly history.

Bec's prom picture topped the others in shock value. Her evening gown showed off a ravishing feminine figure, dipping down her breastbone to reveal her cleavage. She probably considered her powdered white face and dark ghoulish lips goth at the time, but I was so used to the current Bec that she appeared to be done up in women's drag. I felt a twinge of pain for the kid in the photo, or maybe it was a cringe at the thought of myself in such a dress, an outcome I'd escaped by skipping all formal school dances.

As I sat down at the table with my bowl of cereal, the Bec I recognized returned. She had donned Erin's floral dressing gown, still rather drag-like, but with the front loose and open she revealed another colorful tattoo where cleavage had once been. She got both pans on the stove going. Soon the smell of sautéing onions and bacon grease stirred the rest of the house.

Melissa had barely wiped the sleep out of her eyes when she and Bec began trading stories and recollections from the previous night. They entertained me with a dramatic reenactment of

Jess flirting big-daddy style with a girl who may or may not have been of legal drinking age, and acted out a fight between a couple I knew.

When Melissa and I left to pick up coffee, she continued her play-by-play of the night. She spoke for a few nonstop minutes about Bec, using Bec's name repeatedly. "Bec danced on a table . . . a girl untied Bec's shoe . . . Bec bent down and the girl grabbed Bec . . ."

I stopped listening to the story and focused only on grammar and syntax, amazed at what sounded like a tongue twister, all so Melissa could avoid referring to Bec with a pronoun. She used to do the same thing with Pony, the person who lived in my room before me, and I once made the mistake of asking her whether Pony was a he or a she. Melissa had looked at me like I was nuts. "Pony is a pony," she said. Her answer made more sense once I met this fluid and nimble, scruffy person, whom I immediately pictured bending down to toddlers everywhere to sweetly offer pony rides. Pony did look and act as much like a pony as anything else I could name.

I wanted to ask the right way this time, and I was pretty sure now that a person couldn't *be* a pronoun. "So, I have a question for you," I said. A few cars whizzed by as Melissa and I waited at the light at the neighborhood's main intersection. "Does Bec go by 'he' or 'she'? I hear people use both."

"I just call Bec, Bec," she said. "But if you want to know, you should ask Bec."

Disappointed, I'd wanted a definitive answer. Referring to Bec as "he" felt intuitively right, but there were so many rules that linked biology and language, birth sex and pronouns. If Bec intended to override these rules like Greg did, wouldn't she at least adopt a man's name? It felt too absurd for me to refer to a "Rebecca" as "he."

"Let's go," Melissa said, ushering me to cross. The countdown toward *Don't Walk* had already begun. I picked up the pace. On the other side of the street, a swath of light broke through two apartment buildings, casting an unnatural glow onto the sidewalk.

"Who do you think is more butch?" I blurted out. "Me or Jess?"

Melissa turned her head to me, squinting into the light. "More butch?"

"Come on, you know what I mean."

Melissa laughed hoarsely. "Where is this coming from?" She sounded amused and maybe like she felt bad for me.

I told her about the gender spectrum that had been on my mind ever since Jess had dropped it into one of our conversations. I wasn't sure how Jess defined the two poles, and she only focused on the masculine side, but it had a linear order that went Melissa, me, Jess, Bec, and Greg.

Melissa exploded in laughter. "If you get sucked into Jess's world, you're in big trouble. Sometimes I wonder what goes on in that head of Jess's."

"So, your place in the gender spectrum doesn't bother you?"

"Nope."

I looked into her blue eyes, her tight red curls framing a face that strangers "ma'am"-ed most of the time and "sir"-ed some of the time—just like Jess and me. I envied her for not caring about pronouns and spectrums. I couldn't compete with Greg, who considered himself a man, and I couldn't compete with Bec; she was too big, broad, tall, and flat chested, too physically masculine, even when wearing a floral dressing gown. But I couldn't stand the thought of being on the more feminine or womanly side of Jess. "So really, who's more butch?"

I could see the bulldog sign on the coffee shop and the blue and yellow equal sign on the neighboring Human Rights Campaign store when Melissa stopped short and turned to face me. "Nina," she said, her eyes holding both compassion and concern. "You are unique."

It sounded like a euphemism, like calling someone "special." I bowed my head and looked down at my feet, trying to take in her affirmation in that group therapy way. "Like how I'm wearing athletic sandals with socks?" I said. "And sweatpants? In public?"

Melissa clapped her hands together like a kindergarten teacher. "Exactly."

The only other person I knew who would wear gray athletic sweatpants, socks, and soccer sandals in public was my brother. He liked to throw on a sweatshirt too and call the whole outfit a sweatsedo instead of a tuxedo. He wasn't butch at all. He didn't need the word; he was just a guy.

I spotted my favorite local character on the other side of the street walking his lapdog. His long wavy hair flowed down to his ass, and his chest hair sprouted out the sides of his white tank top. He wore leather underwear and leather boots, as he always did on the weekends. I nudged Melissa. "I'm definitely more butch than him, right?"

Melissa cracked up and walked into the coffee shop, leaving me behind with the echo of her laughter. I watched Gay Thor disappear down the block. I was becoming accustomed to the oddities in the Castro, and yet I understood nothing about my place.

A couple weekends later, Saturday afternoon found Jess and me trying to read quietly in the living room. Although we never went to social events together, we had developed a friendship inside our home. We bonded most deeply over our agreement that Erin was a piss-poor roommate. She trailed thongs, latex underwear, and glitter around like breadcrumbs, regularly left her ancient space heater on as if trying to burn down the place, and paid rent according to her own schedule. This afternoon, Erin was chatting loudly into her cell phone as she clomped from room to room, repeatedly opening doors and then slamming them.

Jess lowered her *Vanity Fair* magazine and ran her hand over her head, pulling back her temples along with her black and gray-flecked spikes. She mouthed something I read as, "You gotta be kidding me." I broke into a smile. After a year of required readings by Joan Didion, Richard Rodriguez, and other nonfiction writers, I was so happy to have only independent writing work over the summer and the time to "pleasure read" a novel like *The Virgin Suicides* that even the maelstrom of Erin couldn't bother me.

Sweeping into the living room, Erin plopped into the tattered arm chair and kicked out legs as long as Kansas onto the ottoman. For her burlesque performance later, a blond wig covered her platinum hair and she'd layered herself with a sheer corset, bodice, and evening gown. She inhaled all the air in the room and sighed. "My ex-girlfriend is transitioning," she announced. Her long false eyelashes batted anxiously.

I wasn't sure if it was my recently heightened awareness, the way looking up a word in the dictionary makes it all of a sudden seem to appear everywhere, but it seemed like the reports of name changes, transitions, and top-surgery benefits were constant. Erin was enmeshed in the trans world, but she was also one step removed from the trans guys themselves, so I felt like I didn't have to worry as much about saying the wrong thing and offending her. Seizing the opportunity to hear her perspective, I sat up, placed my open paperback on the armrest of the couch, and egged her on. "Are you surprised she's transitioning?" I asked.

Erin spoke with some frustration about this ex, and I could tell her venting had more to do with their relationship issues and the shock of any Big News than the content in particular. "I'm not really surprised," Erin finally said. "She always hated her body."

I had yet to meet a woman without body image issues. Either her ass was too flat or her ass was too round, her nose too big or her lips too small, her skin tone too light or her areolas too dark. My biggest gripes were my inner tube waist and my excessive body hair, if only because I had to shave constantly to avoid braiding jokes. "Don't we all?"

"I don't," Erin said. I looked at her, taking in the costume that she would soon remove on stage while dancing before a large crowd of people. The thought of taking off my clothes, with or without music, alone in my room was enough for me to want to put on a jacket.

"What's going on?" I asked. I'd been eavesdropping so much that comments like another butch bites the dust and last butch standing were no longer original. "Why are so many dykes doing this?"

Erin wiped underneath her eyes for stray makeup. "I think there's pressure to fit in."

I started to nod, picturing the cliques of trans guys huddled together inseparably at parties and bars, making me think they were passing around the Kool-Aid, when Jess clunked the brick of her magazine onto the antique trunk we used as a coffee table. "I'm not trying to fit in," she said, with an edge to her voice.

"I'm just saying, I think that whatever you are—boi, butch, andro, FTM . . ."

"Do we have to use labels?" Jess cut in.

Using her arms to raise herself, Erin sat up in her chair. "Look, I don't like labels either," she said, a bit defensively.

I resisted my temptation to make a wisecrack about the new "no label" identity. I understood that nobody wanted to be stamped and pigeonholed by others, but labels were also words used to communicate. I thought of Erin as a "high femme," simply as a way of saying that she owned more shoes than I owned books and that her suitcase for a long weekend required a porter. I wished Erin had finished her list. I wanted to know what meanings those other words could hold.

"It's just getting tough for me," Erin said. "I never thought so much about my chest before." She leaned forward, and without much of a rack to hold up her evening gown, the top drooped like an empty bag. "But now that I'm around so many women who hate their tits, I'm all, 'Glue. Them. To. Me.'" She enunciated each word, grasping at her absence.

I too had never before thought much about my chest beyond abstract thoughts of a reduction, but ever since the breast guillotine had gone up like a billboard, it was impossible to avoid what was going on around me.

"You make it sound like all this transitioning is a trend," Jess said. "This, here, San Francisco, it's the only safe space for transitioning, top surgery, any of it."

Erin rose and crossed into the connected kitchen to fill up a glass of water. Walking back, her heels bit into the wood floor. "Well, I'd like to meet a butch who said she let her girlfriend play with her tits last night."

I flipped my baseball cap bill backward and recrossed my legs. "Do all butches really hate their tits?" I asked.

"Probably not," Erin said as she sat back down. She sipped her water. "Just the ones I tend to date."

And just all the ones I heard about, I thought.

"Well, nobody touches mine!" Jess said, tugging on her T-shirt in agitation. "I'm completely dissociated from my tits. They are not part of me. I don't use them for anything."

I stared at Jess, stunned by the force of her statement. In the handful of conversations we'd had about Greg and Bec, she'd never banged the gavel of her feelings so unequivocally. The power of her tone, the frustration underneath, prevented me from calling "bullshit" on her. Yet how could Jess, or anyone, feel disconnected to a body part? It was a conceptual and intellectual riddle that hurt my brain.

An awkward silence hung in the room until eventually Jess rose and went into the bathroom. I thought back to one of my early weeks in the house, Jess standing in front of the bathroom mirror, towel wrapped around her waist, the door wide open. She put in her contact lenses, rubbed lotion onto her face, and applied Crew Fiber to her hair, all the while engaging me in a conversation as if she didn't notice her breasts just flopping around, trailing her as if on time delay, like a poorly dubbed movie in which mouths move but the speech doesn't match up.

At first I pretended not to notice Jess's breasts when she went about her routine. Then I must have actually stopped noticing them. Somewhere along the way, I too started wrapping my towel around my waist after a shower, although I always kept the door to the bathroom closed, not nearly as bold as Jess. Most of what I knew about being a woman, from towel wrapping to bra shopping, came from blindly following my mother or my teammates in the locker room.

But now, living in this house, I had stumbled upon an entire underworld of new information. What those around me had learned from their friends and lovers and gender studies classes in school was foreign to me. I lacked the language that others had acquired through osmosis and theory. Without the words, the ideas—even my experiences themselves, or my understanding of them—had been inaccessible. I felt insatiable and ignorant. "Do you know why Bec had surgery?" I asked Erin, eager to continue the conversation after Jess had left.

She spoke in a lulling cadence, as if telling me a bedtime story. She said Bec had been a rambunctious child who liked to do cartwheels, run around shirtless, and climb trees, all monkey-like and unencumbered. Then puberty came along and changed Bec's body, prevented Bec from doing all those beloved activities.

Erin stopped, as if realizing she didn't have Bec's story right, or it wasn't hers to tell. "You know, you should probably ask Bec about this yourself," she said. "He's very open and would totally talk to you."

I could only imagine how many times Bec had already explained herself to friends, family, and coworkers. Now me, Curious George over here, wanted to know about her body and gender—the most personal and intimate details of her life. I didn't even know Bec's last name or which pronoun to use for her. Unless I was prepared to share with her my own feelings about my breasts, I had no right to ask about hers just because they had been removed. And we weren't close enough friends for chest comparisons, or for me to let on how much I compared mine to hers, from where I stood in the corner, watching.

Three

BINDING

I could've called what I was doing in the downstairs laundry area "window shopping," but really I was snooping. While transferring Jess's clothes from the dryer to her wicker basket to make space for my own, I rooted through her pile in search of her new Title Nine Frog Bra. My soccer playing A-gays raved about the NASA-like engineering that made this sports bra the most functional one on the market, and, used to doubling-up during workouts, I was eager to find a single one that could hold my chest in place. I was also mildly curious about its supposed off-label use, gleaned from overheard conversations—binding. I imagined that was the intent when a few weeks after Jess's declaration of independence from her breasts, Erin gave her one as a gift.

I'd begun poking around the laundry room the second I moved into the house, jumping on my first opportunity to acquaint myself with men's underwear. I'd hold up Jess's "skivvies" or "manties," as she called them, and try to picture them on me. It's how I learned about the various brands and styles—the contour pouch, Y-front, bikini brief. With my unofficial sanction for women to wear men's underwear, I went on a shopping spree. I soon discovered Jess and I had different tastes—she owned pink briefs and leopard-spotted silk ones and I preferred Fruit of the Loom boxer briefs or plaid boxer shorts.

I didn't see the new sports bra in Jess's load and returned upstairs to find her folding clean clothing, an activity so rare that she sometimes slept entwined in a mound of fresh laundry on her bed. I hovered in the entry of her room, sparsely furnished with only a bed, antique bureau, bookshelf that held more reference than reading books, and wooden file cabinet that served as a nightstand. I leaned casually into her doorframe, and asked nonchalantly if she liked the Frog Bra.

Jess fanned out a white undershirt and creased it at the sleeves. "Not really," she said. "It holds my chest too high."

"I'm thinking about getting one," I said. "I hear they're pretty good for working out."

Jess pulled the bra from the cloth cubby in her closet and tossed it underhand to me. "You're welcome to try it."

In the bathroom, I removed my T-shirt and looked in the mirror. In my old loose-fitting sports bra, one of a handful I wore regularly, my breasts merged to form a saggy uniboob, or a lycra-encased sausage. The image was not attractive, but I didn't find my look in an underwire bra, which was more like an over-the-shoulder boulder holder on me, any better. I'd stopped wearing these standard bras due to overstretched straps, and bent clips and wires.

I envied women like my mom, small enough to free-boob it and go braless. I had more than a handful, and my hands were large enough to palm a women's basketball, a men's if it was sticky. Each breast weighed approximately four pounds as measured on a produce scale, although scientific accuracy is questionable because I might have rested too much of my upper body on the scale, rushing before another customer could turn down my grocery store aisle.

For most of my adult life, friends, teammates, and roommates told me I was in denial by claiming a bra size too small. They would all say, "How can you be a C? You can't possibly be a C, because I'm a C." One of my A-gays had even staged a mini-intervention, asking me to prove my size. Wearing a 36-C, I demonstrated that my breasts didn't spill out the sides, the underwire didn't crush the bottoms, and I even dipped forward to show that my breasts didn't accidentally release. My success surprised my friend, but my bras came from solid companies like Maidenform and Bali, not lingerie stores like Victoria's Secret, from which few bras—and no Cs—ever fit me.

Jess and I had similar-size chests, and once I had her Frog Bra on, I understood immediately what she meant: the bra lofted my chest, as well as flattening it. I jumped in place a few times, amazed by the complete lack of bounce. When I put my T-shirt on, I could still make out my curved shape through the cotton, but instead of softballs, I saw baseballs. I forgot about running and athletic function and opened the bathroom door. "I kind of like it," I said.

"You're welcome to have it," Jess replied.

"You're not going to wear it?"

"I don't need it." Jess went back into her closet and emerged with a white sleeveless crop top. "This binder works much better," she said and held it out to me.

Made out of nylon and spandex, the binder had a thick front with multiple layers while the back was transparent and stretchy. It appeared medical, like it might require a prescription, and looked as appealing to wear as a mosquito net corset.

I tried to remember when Jess had traded in her old loose-fitting sports bras, specifically the yellow one with the criss-crossing lines visible through her undershirts, for these binders. Perhaps the change, permanent as she made it seem, had been too recent for me to notice. But before I could ask about her, the desire to see my baseballs downsized to golf balls overwhelmed me. "Can I try it on?" I asked.

"Of course," she replied.

In the bathroom, I left the door slightly open and removed the Frog Bra. I placed my arms through the holes of the tank top and all of the material bunched above the hump of my breasts, digging in like a rubber band with no more give. "There's no way this is going on," I yelled.

"Find the bottom. Pull it down from there," Jess shouted. "Don't worry, it's much easier to get off."

I searched for the bottom, but it was tucked too far underneath the fibrous clump. I took the binder off and started over,
making sure that at least some of the lower edge remained acces-
sible. I gripped a piece near my armpit and slowly began to work
the bottom out. When my arms tired, I dropped them by my sides,
took a deep breath, and then got back to work. Once I'd pulled
the entire lower edge out from the crinkly cluster, I was able to
pull the binder over my breasts. The force pushed all of my flesh
downward, nipples toward stomach, and the binder ended near
the bottom of my rib cage.

I went into my room and found my smallest shirt, collared,
short sleeved, and green with a black horizontal stripe. I'd bought
it used, but it must have originally come from the boys' section of a
department store because of the faded logo, written in a children's
script, that said either "Trans9" or "Trans9." About once a month,
I would try on this shirt as a test, using it the way some women
check their weight fluctuation by trying on their "skinny jeans."
With my Trans9 shirt, I was checking to see if maybe I'd lost a couple pounds and my chest shrunk. I would stand before the mirror
only to see the black stripe expand across my chest, accentuating
my curvature. My mirror needed a warning sign: "Objects in tight
shirts appear larger than you want them to be." I always returned
the shirt to my closet.

With the binder underneath, the Trans9 shirt already felt
looser than usual. I approached the enormous living room mirror
and stepped into the frame. I was shocked. Forget golf balls. I had
flapjacks. It was a sight I never could've imagined. "Goddamn,
I'm cute," I said. I watched my smile spread before I caught Jess's
reflection in the corner of the mirror and blushed.

"It looks really good," Jess said. "Those binders are pretty
amazing."

I nodded, unable to take my eyes off myself. I took a step
closer to the mirror and could see through my shirt the rounded
ledge where my breasts ended. I tried readjusting the flesh, raising
my breasts higher so they were more evenly compressed. Some

extra flab squeezed out by my armpits, but I couldn't see it once I pulled my shirt back down. Although my upper body looked a bit thick, the arch of my chest was subtle, like a slightly warped board. "This binder really is amazing," I said.

Jess went into her room and returned to offer me the full-length version. In the bathroom, I easily peeled off the one I had on. When I pulled the full-length one over my head, even more fabric bunched across the upper part of my chest. "I really don't think this one is going on," I said, grappling to find the bottom. "There's just no way."

"There are larger sizes, but that defeats the purpose," Jess said. "And they stretch."

With my elbows out, I wiggled and wormed. I felt my heat rise, my face flushing. Taking down a small crocodile in the bayou would've been easier than wrestling that thing onto my body. I was lucky I didn't dislocate my shoulder in the process, but eventually I won the fight and headed back into the living room.

"Jesus Christ," I said. "This is warmer than a sweater."

"I don't wear the long ones often," Jess replied. "But they're good underneath dress shirts."

This one compressed my love handles for an added bonus, narrowing me so much that I imagined I could find a tuxedo shirt that fit. All of a sudden, the thought of a wedding invite didn't scare me anymore. By the time I handed Jess her binders back, I was exhausted from the effort of trying them on. She said they came from a website called Underworks, which appeared to sell compression tops and bottoms for after surgeries—just what kinds was unclear—or as cosmetic solutions for males seeking a more masculine shape.

At the time, I cared more about my handsome streamlined reflection than who and what the binders were for, or how much they cost. My contract job at the bank had been extended and for the time being I could afford to spend money, it just required my motivation to override my frugal mentality. Inspired by my boxer brief splurge, the last time I dropped over a hundred bucks at one time and the best impulse decision I ever made, I ordered two tritops and one full-length compression shirt. For sports, and potentially binding, I ordered two Frog Bras from Title Nine to complement the one Jess had given me.

For the next couple months, I wore the tritop binder everywhere. I wrestled it on in the morning before going to work and felt it dig into my skin as I slouched at my desk during the day. When I found time to go to the gym I changed into the Frog Bra, which turned out to be extremely effective for workouts, and after my shower I battled the binder back on in a bathroom stall. I had no problem with strangers seeing me topless, but I didn't want anyone to see the strain on my face, my elbows flying as I fought to squash my breasts in the same careless and aggressive way I might stomp closed an overstuffed suitcase. I understood that women at the gym, women like my mother, women in the workplace—the large majority of women—would consider my actions harmful to all of us as women, or at the very least, harmful to me.

And I was hurting myself. The binder rubbed, scratched, and compressed like a panty-hose tank top; breathing on top of an Andean peak would have been easier. My baseline sweat level rose, especially when I commuted on my bike, so my skin always felt clammy and irritated. My second year of grad school started up at the end of August, and on class days, I'd wear the binder for at least twelve hours. Common sense told me that smashing any part of the human body for such long periods could not be healthy. But every time I caught my reflection in the mirror, I thought to myself, Goddamn, you look good. So, I kept at it, bearing in mind the blisters, twisted ankles, and foot cramps that every woman with stiletto heels or knee-high boots endured for the sake of appearance.

All of my friends noticed my physical change. A straight friend, someone I'd known for years, couldn't get over not just my flat chest, but also the effect it had on my whole presentation. For an entire brunch she kept repeating, "You look so hot, like the boys I date, but cuter." I was flattered, since straight girls, attainable or not, made up my ideal dating pool. One of my A-gays cautiously asked, "Where did your boobies go?" and I could see her relief when I said I was only binding. They all knew about top surgery and binding, even if their knowledge came from Showtime's *The L Word*. Tori, one of my better A-gay friends, asked if I was using an Ace Bandage or duct tape.

I told Tori about the Underworks binders while celebrating an A-gay birthday at a sports bar, the kind of place that catered to both lesbian softball and gay rugby teams. The mixed crowd, as well as the pinball machine, dartboard, and selection of beers on tap made it one of my favorite neighborhood haunts.

"So it's a tank top that just mashes them?" Tori asked.

"It pancakes them but good," I said.

Tori grabbed her breasts and scrunched up her face as if she were a guy who had just gotten nailed in the nuts with a baseball.

I ran my hand down the front of my *Golden Girls* T-shirt, always a Castro crowd pleaser with its sketch portrait of Rose, Dorothy, Blanche, and Sophia. "I think I look great," I said.

"You do." Tori took a sip of her Budweiser, her standard drink even though a martini would've gone better with the business suit she wore from work at a law firm. "So, what happens with this *binder* when you're with the *ladies*?" she rasped.

I had wondered the very same thing. But with my current hook-up rate, about once or twice a year, I wouldn't need an answer for a while. "I'll let you know."

"I'm not sure I'd go home with a girl who wore one of those," she said.

A few claps and hollers came from the stools next to us. Tori howled as well, tapping her beer on the bar. She slapped me on the shoulder and pointed to the Giants game on TV. It had been several years since we'd fought over the sports section of the newspaper, or since I fell for sporty women. Tori reminded me of a professional soccer player I'd once liked, although thankfully, my crush had been a Yankees and not a Giants fan. Just thinking about the night I messed around with that soccer player, I could feel her hand, her mouth, on my breast. I wanted to molt my skin right there in the bar.

I slapped Tori back on the shoulder. "You know, I'm not dying to hook up with someone who's all into my chest," I said.

Tori returned her focus to me. Her tiny features seemed bigger now that she was staring me in the face. "I'm not sure I could date someone who wouldn't let me touch her tits," she said.

"Really, Tori? You dated guys. For many years. They don't have tits."

"Girls. I'm not sure I could date a girl who wasn't into hers."

"Well, then, you and I would never date," I said. "Because I don't want mine."

Tori pressed her thin lips together. I was shocked that her first response was silence instead of her usual defensive antagonism. I was even more shocked that in my frustration, I'd blurted that out with thoughtless ease. When Tori inquired further, I said my chest was large, annoying during workouts, unnecessary since I never planned to breast-feed, potentially cancerous, and I looked better when it was flat anyways. She understood and definitely shared some of those same thoughts, yet she never wished she didn't have breasts at all.

"Don't get rid of your tits, honey," a piercing voice said. Rick, a gay guy and friend of the birthday girl, stuck his head around Tori. His high-pitched voice was even more jarring than usual in combination with his mountain-man beard, newly grown since our last encounter. "I really wanted to be a girl when I was younger," he said. "I used to run around in my sister's dresses." He laughed awkwardly, a shrill rumble that vibrated in my bones. "But then it passed."

"Wait, do you want to be a boy?" Tori asked me.

Ever since Greg's party, it was something I'd asked myself. Imagining being a boy was like trying to envision myself as an alien, or a whale, or maybe Belgian. It was unfathomable. So I kept asking myself, repeatedly, until it was like saying a word over and over until it lost all meaning.

"You're too pretty to be a boy," Rick said.

You sound too much like Pee-wee Herman to dress like Paul Bunyan, I thought. I was annoyed he'd hijacked our conversation and frustrated by his backhanded compliment. I liked being pretty, but I didn't want to be *too* pretty for anything. I certainly didn't want to give up being pretty to be a boy, nor did I want to be told what I could and couldn't be, or should and shouldn't do with my body from a random acquaintance like Rick. "My dad once told me I was too pretty to be a dyke," I countered.

Rick laughed knowingly, as did Tori. We'd all heard that ignorant doozy countless times.

"But really," I said with complete seriousness, my eyes on Rick. "Why would anyone want to be a guy?"

"No joke," Tori said. Catching the bewildered look on Rick's face, she gave him a friendly tension-diffusing squeeze on the shoulder. "But Rick here isn't so bad."

He let out a self-conscious laugh, screechy enough to break glass, before excusing himself to the bathroom. I finished my beer and pushed it away from me. Tori nodded to the bartender, signaled another round, and placed her hand on my back. "I got this one," she said, even though it had been my turn to buy for years.

After experimenting with the tritop binder throughout the summer and early fall, the problems beyond the basic sweating, constriction, and skin irritation had mounted. The bottom part ended near my lower rib cage and rolled up constantly, the annoyance akin to a sock that scrunches down into a shoe. While compressing the upper portion of my torso, the binder foregrounded the padding around my hips, making me feel especially curvaceous. The binder shape also showed underneath T-shirts, as if I had a piece of pliable cardboard wrapped around me, and to be discrete,

I often wore two shirts. On gym days, taking the binder on and off burned so many calories that I could've skipped my actual workout.

Without a doubt, I looked best and felt most confident when flat chested, but I needed some relief from binding. To cut corners, I developed a system. I started to wear the less effective yet more comfortable Frog Bra to the office, figuring nobody there noticed anything about my chest, and I'd already be prepared for the gym. After my postworkout shower, I'd put on a fresh Frog Bra, which I'd keep on when I biked to class in the evenings for sweat control. Upon arrival, I'd go into a bathroom stall and change into a binder, in case there were any cute first-year students to impress. There was one, Ramona, who caught my attention with her sharp comments in our "Classics of Literary Nonfiction" class, but after she dropped the "boyfriend" bomb in casual conversation, I stopped bothering with the binder on class nights.

By October, I was wearing the Frog Bra most of the time and the binder only if I went out on weekends. The less I wore my binders, the more Jess wore hers. Sometimes, she wouldn't even change out of her binder when she got home from a twelve-hour day at the office. One evening, I found her in the kitchen, cooking all her farmer's market vegetables on the verge of spoiling. Steam from the boiling water had fogged up the windows and just seeing the outline of the binder underneath her T-shirt made me hot and itchy.

"How do you do it?" I exploded. "How are you still wearing that binder?"

Jess chuckled as she poured some of her thirty-two-ounce specialty beer from the corner store into a pint glass. I turned down her offer to finish the rest. "I'm serious," I said. "I've been trying those things for the past couple months and they drive me nuts."

Jess leaned back into the crook of the counter. Her laughter gave way to a relaxed smile. "What seems to be the problem?"

I ran through the list of my frustrations, though some didn't apply to Jess since she didn't ride a bike or go to the gym regularly. To prevent the bottom portion of the binder from rolling up, she lifted her shirt to show me a trick. She'd created a crease, folding the bottom, a couple inches of material, back on itself. "It doubles the binder up so it works even better," she said.

I shook my head with a mix of disbelief and admiration. "I still don't know how you do it."

"I find it comfortable."

Comfortable? A bubble bath, a pair of baggy jeans, and fuzzy slippers came to mind. "Comfortable?"

"Look, you can wear a regular bra and have your breasts out there, you can wear a sports bra and have your breasts out there, or you can bind and not have them out there. That's comfortable for me." Jess hopped up on the corner of the counter, settling in for a conversation. I changed my mind about the beer and poured the rest of the bottle into a glass.

"The chest is one of the first places people look to for gender," Jess said. "And I don't want to be associated with anything feminine. When I'm addressed as ma'am or lady, I hate that."

"So, what about 'she'?" I asked. "Are you okay with that?"

"When I hear 'she' I think *who*? Sometimes I look around as if someone else could be there."

I let out a little laugh as I carried my beer across the kitchen and sat on the table next to the stove. "You know Greg calls you 'he'?" I said. The few others who used male pronouns for Jess were in her inner circle. I was not. Jess and I were debate partners, rallying our ideas and questions across the black and white squares of our kitchen floor.

"Hearing 'he' does make me more comfortable," Jess said, washing down the beginning of her smile with a swig of beer. "But I'm only fine with it when it's subversive. I wouldn't want anyone to think I'm a man."

There was only one other option I'd encountered—the gender neutral "ze," which sounded either gender neutered or Russian. I decided to give up on Pronouns 101 until I could find a tutor. There were more important subjects at hand. "So, what do you do with the binder during sex?" I asked.

"I don't take my shirt off." Jess jumped off the counter and took control of the sizzling pan, stirring the mushrooms. "I love breasts. Just not mine. I don't want to see them. I don't want anyone else to see them. When I'm conscious of them, I'm uncomfortable. They don't exist to me. I won't even take my shirt off afterward." She banged the spatula hard on the edge of the pan.

I flinched, momentarily taken aback by her self-assurance. I equated sex—especially relationship sex—with skin-on-skin contact, and I felt sad for Jess, that she'd decided to give that up, go without that kind of intimacy. Then again, I went without sexual intimacy altogether.

Once the force of Jess's assertion settled, I remembered walking past her room while her on-again, off-again girlfriend was in town. Through her door, left ajar for the cat, I saw them in bed together. Jess was on her back, topless. It couldn't have been more than a few months before. I wondered when Jess had stopped taking off her shirt. The power of her conviction made it seem like she'd been keeping herself covered forever. But Jess tended to carve her feelings into stone, whereas I spoke to try on my thoughts and see if they were true. "Sometimes I think about having top surgery," I said.

"Me too," Jess replied. "I'm just not in a position to do it." Her primary reason was her job. She'd already risen high in a company and industry dominated by conservative white men, and she believed that having top surgery could jeopardize her finance career. As a teenager, she'd also had a handful of major surgeries to correct a shoulder injury and still carried the trauma from being hospitalized; she'd recently ended up in a hospital pharmacy so a friend could pick up a prescription, and, overcome with anxiety, she'd had to leave the building and wait outside. "It's not something I'm actively considering," she added.

I had my own concerns about jobs, surgery itself, scarring, society's response, and destroying my parents, but my thinking was mere fantasy, like a dream in which I'd wake up in the morning, my tits gone, and before making coffee I could throw all my bras, sports bras, and binders in the garbage.

"Does this mean you consider yourself trans?" I asked.

"No. To me trans means becoming a man. It's what Greg's doing." Jess opened the cabinet beneath the sink. "Men take up space. They're privileged and entitled. I don't want to be a man!" Her beer bottle clanked into the recycling bin. From the fridge, she removed two Coronas, leftover from a party, opened them both, and handed me one. "Why couldn't I just be a flat-chested dyke?"

I raised my bottle to her in agreement. My top-surgery fantasy had nothing to do with transitioning. Since being a man didn't appeal to me, it seemed like my flat-chested desire had to be straight-up vanity. "It's hard for me to think of top surgery as something other than cosmetic surgery, like a nose job."

"It is essentially cosmetic and I struggle with that," Jess said. "When I read men's magazines, I compare myself to the models. I want to be fit, flat chested, muscular."

I did too. I compared my body to that of men at the gym and on the street, men like my brother, as well as to other boyish dykes. For me, a flat chest was about looking hot. Even on a lesbian show like *The L Word*, both the androgynous and the transgender characters were super flat chested; it was hard to pull off an attractive masculine aesthetic with huge breasts. I often caught other dykes wishing aloud for narrower hips, flatter chests, bigger muscles— markers I associated with physical masculinity. It was frustrating to think I'd escaped the influence of mainstream beauty only to fall for media-inspired standards in a flipped alternative universe.

"It is cosmetic," Jess repeated. She focused on her stir-fry, tossing the vegetables with great contemplation. Sweat beaded near her hairline and she wiped her forehead with her arm. "But it's more than that. It's about identity."

She looked up at me, her pale cheeks rosy from the heat. I

could tell she was waiting for me to agree or object, but I had no response, let alone an identity—if the gender pronounced at birth wasn't a given, I wasn't sure where to find one. But I agreed with Jess, something about top surgery had to go deeper than the surface. War-wound-size scars weren't cosmetically beautiful.

Outside of my house, I wouldn't have shared my comparison of top surgery to face lifts and nose jobs with anyone—that was best left to health insurance companies. I had read a few articles on trans issues here and there, and I knew that too many people desperate to change their bodies and unable to afford surgery went to chop shops or committed suicide. I felt guilty Jess and I were having a comfortable, intellectual discussion, as if we were in a seminar at one of our fancy liberal arts schools, about something she could easily pay for herself, and that I, if I kept working, probably could eventually, as well. We weren't desperate.

Or maybe we were and just didn't know it, refusing to accept the extent of our struggle because we had to live it. I continued to favor the Frog Bra and wear the binders as little as possible. If having breasts was such a burden that I'd call a chafing, sweaty, constricting, irritating chest girdle "comfortable" like Jess did, I was in trouble. I couldn't wear those binders forever, and I couldn't think about where I'd be forced to go and what I'd have to confront if I let myself love the image of the flat-chested person in the Trans9 shirt. It was easier to try to avoid mirrors and my own reflection, to look away.

Four

MIDDLE GROUND

Despite the record-breaking Indian summer heat, I tried to turn down the invitation to the A-gay pool party. It was across the Bay, on the far side of the Oakland hills, at someone's parents' house. I argued that there was no public transportation escape route and gave in only when Zippy, in town for an appointment with her family dentist, texted me, "Get your ass over here. Pronto." Used to my one-foot-out-the-door ways, she suggested I bring my bicycle on my ride's car rack so I could pedal to the nearest train station at any moment. Her solution was perfect, even though I hadn't shared the real cause of my anxiety, that my chronic bathing-suit phobia might escalate into a full-on bathing-suit panic attack.

Sometimes I thought I moved to San Francisco, or at least stayed, because the coastal fog and cool summer made a jacket and wool hat required beach attire. Back when I broke the men's underwear seal, I also purchased a pair of Billabong swim trunks, a baggy, knee-length revelation that at least made half of my body bearable in sunny weather. Hiding my top business was still a challenge, my discovery of binders useless for lounging by a pool. With only two options, I chose my more water-appropriate Speedo racing top over the Frog Bra, as if appropriateness mattered when wearing a makeshift bathing suit.

The second my trunks were on, my tropical daydream hit, as if there was magic dust in the mesh lining. In it, I'm running on a white sand beach, completely alone. With the sun beating down on my bare back, my legs are spinning and my arms pumping. As I speed along the shore, weaving in and out of the waves, my breasts are weightless, buoyant as helium balloons.

In my room, I removed my shirt and held the flesh on my chest, trying to replicate the sensation of lightness as if I could alchemize breasts into feathers. I walked over to the mirror and noticed the fat squeezing through the openings in my fingers. I pressed myself in tighter and tried to envision myself without boobs. It didn't work. I looked like I was wearing a bra made out of human hands, which although creepy was way better than the Speedo racing top. This provided coverage but was looser than I desired, leaving me with my uniboob sausage. I quickly put on my tank top and mentally padlocked it.

Two A-gays, my bike, and I arrived to a dozen or so scantily clad athletic women milling around the pool. Surveying the bikini fest from the upper deck of the house, I thought I was watching an early scene from *Girls Gone Wild,* except the girls had a dykey strut, shouted instead of spoke, and hadn't yet gone wild. I spotted two boys, the host's college-aged brothers, and wondered if they felt out of place, as if they'd been mistakenly given VIP access to a club.

Across a patch of perfectly manicured grass, there was a Ping-Pong table and a basketball half-court. Beside the pool, a hot tub was tucked into the corner underneath the shade of trees. I was already glad to be there; access to this kind of property was rare. I set up camp at a round table where Tori and a few others were playing dominos, and added my Sunday *New York Times* and *Details* magazine to the leisure reading pile on top of *Bitch* and *Bust* magazines.

Zippy scampered over for our reunion. Since Ta-Ta Tatas, we hadn't seen each other or even spoken for more than a few minutes, maybe once or twice—the emerging reality of a long-distance friendship. I was happy to see her face, yet well aware that large groups overstimulated her, and I had little expectation of one-on-one time. I also had no idea where to begin with someone so far removed from my daily life. "It's hot as balls out here," I said.

"Hot as your mama," she replied. "What's that I hear?" she

cupped a hand to her ear. "What, what . . . is that the pool calling your name?"

I shrugged her off with a laugh. It was too early in the afternoon to start making swimming excuses.

Zippy handed me a bottle of SPF 4 sunscreen. "Help a sister out," she said, kneeling between my legs. A tanning professional, known to wear a bikini under business casual work wear as well as being a regular visitor to the spray-tan booth, Zippy was an even brown.

She brushed her hand up my leg and I jerked it away. "Holy moly," she shouted. "Somebody stopped shaving."

Squirming uncomfortably in my seat, I felt the plastic slats sticking to the back of my thighs. In the past month, my legs had gone from a stubbly cheese grater to a plush felt rug, the softness a sensation that I preferred. I told myself that I hadn't stopped shaving intentionally; it was more that every time I saw my disposable orange razor in the shower, I couldn't find any reason to pick it up. "Well, it's not like anyone ever sees my legs." I hoped my face wasn't as red as it felt.

Tori, sitting in the seat next to me, leaned over to see. "Good god." She pinched an inch of hair between her fingers. "That's no excuse."

I scowled at her and shook my head, a useless chiding. Tori had two modes, completely supportive and utterly obnoxious, and only she controlled the switch. "Are you falling under the influence of those roommates of yours?" she pushed.

"So what if she is?" Jane said, eyeing me with support from across the table. I loved Jane. Her history extended well beyond this small homogenous circle and included all types of people. With her wavy dirty-blond hair, she reminded me of a gorgeous golden retriever, and she was more androgynous than the other A-gays, even in her bikini. She raised a leg to the glass table. "I don't shave, either."

"You have no hair," Tori said. "And it's blond."

I appreciated Jane's effort to back me, even though I had more hair on my big toe than she had on her whole body.

"Well, Nina can do whatever she wants," Jane said, holding me with her gaze. "Right, honey?"

I nodded in agreement and flashed Tori a fake smile that didn't quite mask my embarrassment. The power of her barbs came from the underlying truth in them—my roommates *were* influencing me. I thought about Bec, her recent complaint about her silky dolphin skin, her desire for at least a few wisps of ruggedness. At first, I didn't believe that a female, even a boyish one, could want body hair, but with her voluntary mastectomy, Bec was unlike anyone I'd ever met. When I nervously showed her the happy trail on my stomach, the thin line of hair that had been waxed and shaved in shame dozens of times, she said, "Dude, that's so cool," and rubbed my stomach as if I were Buddha. For a second, I felt proud. That was around the time I stopped shaving my legs.

"Hey, missy," Zippy said. "Easy on the sunscreen."

There was a huge puddle of white on her upper back. "Right. God forbid you avoid skin cancer," I said sarcastically. I started to massage her back, lifting one bikini strap and then the other, rubbing underneath until the white disappeared. I applied some more lotion to her lower back and snuck my fingers underneath the elastic waistband of her low-cut bottoms. I felt awkward and clumsy, envisioning myself as my brother helping the pretty girls with their sunscreen on our scuba-diving adventures. I wondered if anyone was watching me. I concentrated hard on not missing a spot. Then I patted Zippy's back, sending her off. "You're all set, pal."

I kept busy to avoid the pool, flipping though *Details*, snacking on chips, salsa, and strawberries. I ate constantly in case I needed to claim the thirty-minute rule to avoid cramping while swimming. I played a few games of Ping-Pong until the game switched to beer pong. I moved constantly and fell into a steady cycle of drinking water, having a beer, and heading up to the house to use the bathroom.

In the late afternoon, it was still too hot to walk on the cement barefoot, and after a few beers, I did hear the pool calling my name. I actually enjoyed swimming, but like lactose-intolerant people who fought the urge to eat ice cream, I fought the desire, knowing the outfit required would leave a pit of sickness in my stomach.

I walked over to the basketball hoop and picked up the slightly deflated ball. Nothing relaxed me more than the cadence of a basketball rhythmically hitting the ground. The steady sound of a bounce, a swish, a bounce, a swish, was like meditation. I scissored my legs, passed the ball through, and tapped it into the hoop off the backboard.

The host's two brothers joined me on the court and we took turns trading shots. Both shirtless and sculpted with muscles, the younger one was a swimmer with the abs and deltoid wings to prove it, and the older one was thicker with a weight lifter's bulk. I admired their ripped chests, the hump of their biceps as they launched, elbow bent for a jump shot. They suggested a game of H-O-R-S-E, and although it took longer than it should have, I knocked them both off. We shook hands and I cut back across the grass to the pool.

Several of the A-gays had been watching and hailed my return with high fives, "good jobs," and something about kicking boy ass. "Get your sharp-shooting guns into this pool," Tori shouted from a raft in what for her passed as an apology.

I said I'd be back in a minute and climbed the stairs to the house. I opened the sliding-glass door to the remodeled kitchen. Zippy followed me in, shutting the door behind us. The air-conditioning blew the smell of baking brownies around the room. Zippy took her Gatorade bottle out of the fridge. "You really squashed those guys," she cackled.

I barely smiled, trying to play it cool. I liked the attention of winning, regardless of whether it was against men, women, or toddlers. I poured myself a glass of water and leaned over the countertop, scanning the scene outside. A crowd was forming around a patio table that boasted bowls of potato salad, pasta salad, and corn.

"Look at them," Zippy continued, gesturing toward the boys, now hanging around the edges of the A-gays in bikinis working the grill. She opened a container of vanilla cake frosting on the counter and scooped some up with her finger. "I bet they love all these hot chicks at their house."

Watching the two guys reminded me of a scene from a high school health class video: the moment when the pimply adolescent boy climbs up to the high dive at the public pool. He looks out at all the bare skin and cleavage, and then pops a huge boner, blushing a cartoonish stoplight red. "I bet it's a little uncomfortable for them," I said. "Our friends are hot."

"Hells yeah, we are," Zippy said, dipping for more frosting.

"Everyone here is really hot," I repeated quietly to myself, not expecting to be heard.

"No shit, Sherlock," Zippy said.

I watched the A-gays through the sliding door, their conversation muted by the glass. I'd always found them attractive; I'd never thought much of it. Now it weighed on me. I felt myself searching for something I couldn't articulate. "Everyone is hot," I repeated again.

Zippy held her wet, glistening finger in the air, her widening eyes nudging me.

I glanced at the tile floor and when I looked back at her, I saw it clearly. She was a woman. And I was not. It made no sense. I turned back to the floor.

"Duh," she said. "We're hot."

We weren't. *She* was and *they* were. But *I* wasn't. I could've had their bodies. I could've worn a bikini. I had worn a bikini. I could've waxed and shaved and tanned. I had done all three. I had looked exactly like them. Maybe I still did look like them. To Zippy, I was one of them. Hot. But to me, looking like them, no matter how attractive I found them, made me feel ugly. I understood then, fully and completely, I wasn't an A-gay, or a woman-loving-woman, or a lesbian—capital-L or not. I'd never pass the entrance exam. I wouldn't even sit for the exam.

I thought back to the weekend I'd gone away with some of them to Portland, three summers before, crashing at their hotel for a campy lesbian soccer tournament. I hadn't brought a bathing suit, and yet I wanted to be included so badly that I went into the hot tub in my black bra and underwear—now packed away in a cardboard box with other items from a different era: my VCR, cassette tapes, and additional objects I held on to in case the digital revolution was just a phase. How hard I'd tried to pretend I fit in; I'd fooled all of my A-gays and they accepted me, they let me be one of them. They considered me safe, part of the collective, subsuming me under a group that now made me feel paralyzed, as if I couldn't move or speak with this womanhood hovering over me.

I saw myself most clearly in the brothers outside, in my own brother, in the teenage boy in the old health class video, and yet I was not like any of them at all. I'd played in those lesbian soccer tournaments, traveled to the Sydney Gay Games for basketball and soccer, lived in my college rugby house, lettered in five high school sports, all with women. Those experiences, my camaraderie with these women, were my greatest joys. My awareness and incomprehension rendered me speechless. Zippy licked the last trace of frosted sugar off her finger, and I left her in the kitchen to bounce off the walls.

When I returned outside, everyone was still eating or passed out by the side of the empty pool. I dipped my foot over the ledge. The sun was falling fast, a grayness settling on the water. As I started to remove my tank top, Stephanie stirred on her nearby towel.

"Finally," she said, sitting up. She adjusted the triangles of her bikini. "We'll be able to see who has a bigger chest."

Word of my size complaints must have gotten around, mangled by the A-gay game of telephone. I tucked my elbow back into my shirt.

"Oh, come on," she taunted playfully. "You think you've got a big chest? Let's see who has something to show off."

Stephanie was a loud, brash leader, the captain when it came to soccer and always a competitor. She was the kind of person who'd try to carry all her grocery bags up to the house in one trip even if it left marks on her arms and wrists, just for the challenge. She pulled her shoulders back and pushed her chest forward, not with feminine pride, but tomboy pride, for being able to play sports, scuffle, do anything and everything physical, while also owning large, sexy breasts. Like the other A-gays, Stephanie fought not only to be strong but also to be a strong woman.

I felt no allegiance to her side in us versus them, and I was done comparing breasts, done listening to, "You're not a C because I'm a C," done engaging in the party game where a blindfolded person tries to guess who everyone is by feeling their chests, done likening myself to other women. Still reeling from my epiphany in the kitchen a few minutes before, I felt anger rise in me. "It's not about whose chest is bigger," I said with controlled intensity. "I complain because I don't want mine at all. And I've been waiting all day for a quiet moment to swim. So, please, please, can you let me do so in peace."

Back-pedaling apologies tumbled from her lips. I calmly explained that I wasn't upset with her; she'd had no idea how I felt. Until I asserted myself to her, I hadn't realized the power of my own feelings, nor my ability to express them with some composure. For a brief moment, my confidence displaced my physical discomfort. Empowered, I stripped off my shirt and entered the pool from the steps on the shallow end.

The water was colder than I'd anticipated. I could feel goose bumps prickling up on my skin. To warm myself, I did a few breaststroke laps, keeping my head above the water, watching the waves ripple away from me in tiny splashes. I flipped onto my back and floated, still and alone, with only the occasional shout or laugh from the upper deck breaking the silence.

I stayed at the party until the very end, when my same friends drove me home, my unused bicycle back on the roof rack.

After the pool party, I decided not to talk about my body or gender issues with my A-gays. They didn't get it. The problem was I didn't know what "it" was, and so I didn't get "it" either, and I needed to understand something, anything, even if it was why I was becoming so fixated on my chest. Whenever I walked past mirrors, my attempts to avert my eyes only lured me back into the frame, and at work, I found myself taking unnecessary pee breaks as excuses to steal extra glances at myself.

If I was wearing a binder and shirt, my reflection would ask me, "Can you see your breasts? Are they too big? Do they look funny? Can other people see them? If you were less neurotic, could you let this go?" If I was topless, either before or after a shower, I'd scrutinize my breasts themselves, searching for an identifiable problem. From above, they looked like rockets about to crash or like a pair of socks weighed down with coins—could my annoyance be caused by the sag, or my stretch marks? And why did my nipples seem, I don't know, too nippley? Occasionally, when I wasn't deep into one of my investigations, I'd peek quickly, catch myself head-on. "Nice rack," I'd think, before all my synapses could fire and connect the rack to me.

When I wasn't obsessing over my boobs, I was reading about gender. I substituted my "Classics of Literary Nonfiction" books with my own "Classics of Transgender History" reading list. Of course, the trans-themed book list was short, which made almost anything on it a classic. I breezed through Jamison Green's *Becoming a Visible Man*, recommended by someone at the gay bookstore in my neighborhood as the most informative transsexual narrative, and then turned to Leslie Feinberg's *Stone Butch Blues*.

I was in the living room reading the semiautobiographical novel when Bec came in, fresh from an afternoon nap. She yawned and stretched her long arms overhead before her eyes landed on the book cover. "Tough read," she said, curling into the love seat.

"No joke," I replied. The story was not only painful but personally scary. If Bec and I had been born in a different era when laws enforced gender-appropriate clothing, a bad night at the dyke bar would've meant a beat-down and a jail cell, whereas I considered no new phone numbers and the spins something to whine about.

"Sometimes I wonder how many butch and trans people killed themselves back then." Bec untucked her legs from her chest, planted her feet on the ground, and sat up tall, spreading her broad shoulders like a butterfly. "I wonder how many suicides there are even now," Bec said. "I'm lucky."

I spoke directly into the target of her chest. "Lucky?"

"There's a lot of people desperately seeking top surgery. I was able to do it. Though I'm still paying for it. Probably will be for a while."

She interlocked her fingers between her knees and leaned forward, encouraging me with her openness. "Why did you do it?" I asked. "If you don't mind talking about it?"

"I don't mind." Bec headed to the kitchen and offered me a Bud Light, which I declined. "Gotta maintain my girlish figure," she joked as she slithered a hand down the side of her hip. She dropped back down into the love seat, her Gumby-like frame filling a space made for two, and placed her bottle by her foot. "What I did was a big deal. I removed a huge part of what the world views as Woman."

Without much prodding, Bec told me about her decision-making process, and it revolved, to my surprise, entirely around her body, not her gender. She said she didn't know what would've happened had she ended up with a B-cup rather than a DD, but she couldn't be bothered to speculate on the what-if. Ever since her breasts showed up, she'd found everything about the look and feel to be unattractive, uncomfortable, and unhealthy. They caused zits and sweat in the creases. They were a risk for cancer. They acted as an annoying barrier to snuggling up to girls in bed. They were weird, saggy, and gross, stage props with a use and purpose she never understood.

She'd always fantasized about their disappearance, imagining a breast reduction to nothingness. In her early twenties, being in queer spaces, she discovered that people did remove breasts entirely. Lack of money prevented any serious consideration, and then she entered a long-term relationship with a lesbian and thought it selfish to make a change to her body, especially with joint funds.

Bec moved to North Carolina with this girlfriend, and a year and a half later, when their breakup became imminent, Bec planned a return to San Francisco. This major life transition presented the perfect time for a major physical change. What had always been in the background of Bec's mind leapt to the forefront. She searched online, using words like *breast reduction, gay,* and *queer,* until she acquired the terminology, words like *top surgery, bilateral mastectomy, female-to-male, transgender*—the latter a word she hadn't considered applying to herself at the time. Bec found a website that housed a repository of before-and-after surgery pictures from a variety of doctors. Nothing she saw on those pages was worse than the baggage she carried on her own chest. Bec repeatedly concluded the best results came from the San Francisco–based Dr. Brownstein, a talented and well-respected surgeon, and one of only a few who performed the procedure.

I'd learned from my readings that the "top surgery" everyone around me threw out so casually was considered by the medical community to be gender reassignment surgery—a step in the transition from woman to man. Doctors, regarding this surgery as a treatment for Gender Identity Disorder, followed a set of recommended ethical guidelines, which included a psychological permission slip. But Bec didn't appear to be sick, and as far as I could tell, she wasn't transitioning from woman to man. "How'd you get around the therapist's note?" I asked Bec.

"Brownstein asked me how long I'd been living as a man," Bec explained. "I said a year and a half. That's how long I'd been in North Carolina where everyone thought I was a guy. If it walks like a duck and talks like a duck, then maybe it's a . . ." she trailed off.

I cocked my head, waiting for her to finish the phrase, but she shrugged her shoulders. She wouldn't claim herself as a man, or male, being one or becoming one either. That she'd bypassed medical community guidelines left me unfazed, but I was astonished that she'd trusted her top-surgery desire without any intention of "being a man"—that was the only accepted reason I'd ever heard to pursue a flat, streamlined chest.

There had to be something Bec wasn't telling me. Like a prosecuting attorney, I tried to trick her into stating her manhood. I asked why she always "packed" a huge noticeable bulge in her briefs and she said it was because she liked her reflection, not because men had bulges. Every aspect of her physicality, from her natural height to her flat chest and large package, screamed man, and yet Bec, sitting across from me in her pink-and-black T-shirt, her women's flag-football uniform, didn't consider herself one.

She lived as a seahorse, an identifying animal she threw out, and not for the reason I expected—the anomalous male "pregnancy" or brood pouch—but rather for the fact that seahorses change coloration in adaptation to their surroundings. "Some people would call me genderqueer," Bec said. "I don't use that term, but I do think of myself as occupying the middle ground."

I loved the way that sounded, like the best of both genders, a compromise. I wished our culture, language, and public bathroom situation allowed a person to hold elements of man and woman at the same time.

"The middle ground must pose problems for you," I said, emboldened by Bec's frankness. "I notice people refer to you with both pronouns. Do you have a preference?"

"I do prefer 'he,'" Bec said. "But 'she' is easier and makes the most sense to a lot of people. So, really, either is fine."

I was one of those people for whom it was easier. It had taken me so many months to pose such a simple question, but underneath my inclination to ask was the willingness to let go of the rules and reconfigure a training so ingrained it felt hardwired. And this was not simple. Allowing a person to make a choice, especially a confusing choice like linking "Rebecca" with "he," threatened the entire foundation of gender as permanent, given, and obvious. This might've still been scary had I not felt so free. I wanted to refer to Bec as "he," his clear preference, and to uncover terms like *genderqueer* and *middle ground* that articulated what I thought I could see but not explain—that there were more identities and people under the category of transgender than just transsexuals, those who transition from female to male or from male to female, making those other terms real. Making them possibilities for me.

"Do you ever consider testosterone?" I asked Bec.

"T is not something I've ruled out, but it's not something I want to jump into," Bec said. "And I'm a little concerned my career could push me further into man territory." Interested in working in trauma settings, he recognized that a medical emergency is not an ideal time to confuse others with his androgyny, and that looking like an adolescent boy could scare someone whose life he's trying to save.

For now Bec was content in the middle and with himself. I was amazed that he managed to do it, though, exist in a realm that to most people didn't exist, and do it with such grace. I pictured him on Canada Day, floating around my kitchen with the maple-leaf flag as his dance partner, his ease and glide visible in every step. "Were you always this comfortable with yourself?" I sputtered with incredulous reverence. "Or was it a process for you?"

A smile opened on Bec's porcelain face and he crossed his legs effeminately. "Oh, it was a process," he said. "A metamorphosis. Although I don't know what I'm metamorphing into."

I yearned for his physicality, for the unobstructed energy that flowed through his every action. I thought myself foolish to believe that by shedding my chest I'd be able to escape the heaviness of my head, to achieve such bodily elegance. But that's what I saw in Bec—the bars stifling my movement raised, my straitjacket slipped off. I wanted his freedom, independent of gendered terms, although I had the sense that language itself created some of the space. I also had the sense that his lightness could be mine and that all that weighed me down was a measly eight pounds.

In mid-November, two weeks after his top surgery, Greg showed up at Melissa's birthday party at my house wearing a yellow collared shirt about two sizes smaller than any shirt I'd ever seen on him. Even from across my back deck, he looked less beefy and more agile, as if he'd switched from the offensive line to the defensive line in football. He stood loosely, his arms hanging by his sides, his shoulders tilted back.

I congratulated Greg with a hug, wrapping my arms awkwardly around him so as not to press myself into his upper body. I asked how he was feeling, and when he replied with a dull, inexpressive "fine," I hovered, hoping that he might share more information with his better friends as they greeted him with similar sideways hugs. One of his flag-football teammates asked to see his chest and I couldn't believe it when he enthusiastically agreed. I considered any "show us your tits" request inappropriate, which made "show us the site of your lopped off tits" seem doubly inappropriate. Six months after Ta-Ta Tatas, and I still needed to switch into the mind-set of the breast guillotine as blessing and not humiliation.

Greg opened up his show-and-tell invitation to anyone in earshot, and I jumped on the back of the three-person train following him. "We can go in my room," I offered, but Greg led us into Jess's room instead and shut the door behind us. We all formed a close circle around him and he lifted up his shirt. A large elastic wrapping, like an Ace Bandage, covered his chest from his sternum to his stomach, raggedly cut underneath his armpits. Julie, an artsy tomboy with do-it-yourself dyed hair tucked under a vintage baseball cap, helped him unlatch the Velcro in the back. "How long do you have to wear this?" she asked.

"Only a couple more days," Greg said.

He'd already completed the hardest part, the first five days with drains, small tubes that carried excess fluid from his chest into grenade-like receptacles. He'd already had the stitches removed from the nipple grafts. He'd started showering again, his back to the water stream. He'd returned to regular hours at work.

I knew all the details regarding the pre-op appointments, three-hour outpatient procedure, and two-week recovery from talking with Bec and then checking out Dr. Brownstein's information-rich website afterward. With a few clicks, I'd found the mother lode of top-surgery pictures, and in the privacy of my own room, I looked at dozens of poorly lit and often headless before-and-after pictures, all too clinical to be appealing. They reminded me of the before-and-after teeth-whitening photos on the wall of a dentist's office, where it's hard to focus on the results since I'm too disgusted by the close-up of a stranger's mouth, teeth, and gum line.

But this was no anonymous, mute stranger before me. It was Greg who, in two days, would chuck the white bandage in the trash. There'd be no more doubling up with Frog Bras and binders—no more strangled chest, shortness of breath, rashy skin. It would soon be over. Forever. My joy for him was mixed with jealousy, my curiosity charged with anticipation. I tapped my foot on the wood floor, waiting for Julie to unlatch the Velcro on Greg's bandage.

Underneath, white protective tape crossed over patches of gauze on Greg's nipples to form asterisks. A few inches below, two sets of small diagonal lines, patterned like the stitching on a football, stretched horizontally across his chest.

With Julie holding his shirt up for him, Greg painstakingly lifted the tape, his skin sticking ever so slightly to the adhesive. He removed the gauze from his right side to reveal the healthy rosy pink of his nickel-size nipple.

"Oh my god, so cute," Adina squealed. "Your nipples are so cute."

A "pretty boy" with a taste for designer clothes and highlighted hair, Adina was also a motorcycle-riding, hard-nosed athlete and could tear up the dance floor in "umptse-umptse" gay boy clubs. I'd known her for years, but only recently had I come to see her as effeminate, kind of faggy, actually.

"You're so handsome," she said with a hint of friendly flirtation.

Greg's cap, cocked to the side, shaded his flushed cheeks. "I think I'm blushing," he said, trying to keep a straight face as Adina, Julie, and Hillary drowned him in praise. "I can't believe I'm blushing."

My excitement had faded to a disappointed detachment. Greg's redesigned chest, clearly created by a skilled hand, looked just like that, a redesign. The only one in the room who hadn't spoken, I could only gesture my support with nods.

"So cute," Julie reiterated, and in a half-joking yet serious manner added, "and so very manly."

The first time I'd observed this type of gender reinforcement, a few women cooing over someone's testosterone-fueled mustache growth, I found it forced and childish, almost unbearable, like listening to adults tell a young girl wearing a pink dress, rhinestone necklace, and holding a wand that she is a princess. But Greg had worked hard, fought for his gender and body. With his elbows out, holding his shirt up, he tried to remain still, but his childlike glee lit up his face like fireworks. Delight shot off of him, prying my mouth open to boost his pride. "You look awesome," I said. The smile on Greg's face flickered brighter and I felt a rush of pleasure. "Really awesome," I repeated.

I couldn't see past the tiny red lines, the threadlike scabs that surrounded his nipple graft, and the obviousness of the reconstruction made an indelible mark in my mind. I found breasts, even my own, more attractive than cuts and scars, and yet it took nothing away from me to support Greg.

Everyone kept telling him how great he looked in a grand chorus, and inspired by the solidarity, I contributed to the encore until
Greg couldn't take it anymore. "Now I just gotta lose this beer gut,"
he said, slapping his stomach.

Julie helped wrap the bandage back around his chest. "How
tight should this be?" she asked.

"Oww," Greg groaned, sucking in his stomach in agony. "Just
kidding."

Julie let out a relieved smile. "Jerk," she said, closing the Velcro and pulling his shirt down.

"High five. High five," Adina said. She held out her hand,
which Greg met in a low handshake.

The only person I barely knew in the room was Hillary. She
played flag football with the others, often with her blond hair in
pigtails, sporting the ironic phrase "The Butch One" on the back
of her uniform. She held her shirt up, her fingers poised underneath her turquoise bikini. "I guess I have to take this off," she
joked.

"How long do you have to wear that?" Greg deadpanned.

Hillary reached around her back and pulled the string. Standing there, her chest on display, unlike Greg, she didn't blush.

"I think you have the greatest tits I've ever seen," said Adina,
sounding sincere. "Really, you do."

"It's always nice to see your tits, Hillary," Greg said. He
helped her retie her bikini in the back and turned to Adina. "Your
turn."

Adina had once expressed a desire to be completely flat chested
to me, but as it was, I could barely make out bumps through her
faded gray T-shirt. I would've killed or at least maimed for her
small boy boobies. She raised her shirt and lifted her tight Frog
Bra. We all nodded in seeming approval, knowing enough to treat
her display as a nonevent, as if she'd shown us her feet.

"Next," Greg said, shifting to Julie.

Julie shook her head sideways. "Nope. I never take off my
clothes."

Greg shrugged and cocked his head at me with a playful grin. "Come on, Nina," he said. "Last one."

After Julie, I had an easy out, a pass. But as I looked around at the person with girly breasts, baby-boy breasts, no-more breasts, and no-show breasts, I realized breasts could be what we wanted them to be. Mine didn't have to be the most revered part of the female form; they could just be hunks of flesh, at least among the people surrounding me. I took a step forward, bringing myself fully into the circle, and lifted my T-shirt and Frog Bra to indifferent nods.

"Next showing will be at three," Greg said, turning to the door.

I followed the trail out of the room, invigorated by the possibility of reinventing my own body. The meaning was mine, as long as I was with those who had the vision and vocabulary to understand my creation. I closed the door behind me, feeling lighter already.

Five

PACKING

Jess entered the frame of the large living room mirror, grabbed her crotch, and readjusted the bulge in her jeans. "What do you think, Roscoe?" she said in the high-pitched voice she reserved for her cat. "Should Papi pack tonight?"

"Yes, Papi should pack," I squeaked back from behind my book. Jess always greeted Roscoe before me and I rarely missed my chance to ventriloquize a reply.

Aware that drag kings packed for performances, some women might do it to be subversive or ironic—I once saw a girl bunny packing at the annual Hunky Jesus Easter event—and some trans guys did it to physically embody their identities as men, I imagined Jess got her soft silicone packer a couple years before, along with latex gloves and leather cuffs, as part of the queer starter kit—items used to explore aspects of sexuality that often went unacknowledged during adolescence. I must have been on the road when my kit was offered, and I had been satisfying my experimental curiosity by observing Jess, who'd been recently engaging in this mirror routine.

Pivoting on the heels of her sturdy black boots, she held the remnants of a smile on the corners of her lips. "Do I look girly in these jeans?" she asked.

For the past couple months, every time Jess went out with Greg and Bec, she packed. Although she said it was part of being boys together, her question made me think there was more to it. Her baggy, ripped jeans with their round of denim near the fly hinted at guy, and yet they still lacked the hip-slenderizing, thigh-minimizing, ass-shrinking buttons she desired. I pushed hers for her, telling her what I would've wanted to hear. "No, not at all."

"I just started bleeding," she said. "I feel gross."

Ever since Jess had told me her hormones didn't make her a woman, I'd been noticing her avoidance of words like menstruate, period, and PMS, as if she'd specifically chosen the word *bleeding* to capture her body's physiology while keeping her distance from women.

"That sucks," I said. "Bleeding fucks me up too. Makes me feel all voluptuous." I faked a gag.

"Hey, why don't you come out with us?" Jess said, as if the idea had just occurred to her.

"I don't know," I said. "The Boys" were nice enough to me in my own home, and I enjoyed one-on-one conversations with each, but when I bumped into them out I barely registered on their social radar. They always went to the same dive and turned into just another clique at a bar that reminded me of a high school cafeteria, a place where everyone acted territorial and insecure. "I'm not sure I can handle the scene."

"We're taking it easy. It's Saturday night and aren't you on winter break?"

With only six weeks of freedom before I'd be forced back to Thoreau, I was ripping through the trans treasure trove. Jess's eyes settled on the cover of my book. "*How Sex Changed: A History of Transsexuality in the United States,*" she droned.

"It's a little dense, but you wouldn't believe the shit that's in here. It's very historical. You'd actually love it." I told her about Christine Jorgensen, the first transsexual media sensation back in the early 1950s whose publicity opened the floodgates of possibility; after the story of her transition from male to female broke, she received thousands of letters from people who identified with her. Given the media storm surrounding Jorgensen, it was a near conspiracy neither Jess nor I had learned about her before. "We can thank her story for bringing us the term . . ." I threw up some mocking air quotes, *"sex-change operation."* Both Jess and I knew there was no one special operation and certainly no dick fairy— bottom surgery for trans guys was rare, expensive, and the results less than ideal.

"Put the book down and come out with us," Jess said.

Of all The Boys, it was Jess I'd struggled the most with in social settings—she simply ignored me. Or maybe I ignored her, disinterested in her puffed-up public persona. But lately, our conversations about gender were bringing us closer. As part of our ongoing personal investigations, we'd fallen into a knowledge-share. I'd tell her about transgender history, pathology, and theory from my self-assigned reading list; she'd tell me about binding, packing, and gender bending as it was practiced. She readjusted her bulge again. I stared, embarrassed by my transparency, my eagerness to discover what was beyond my books and absorb what Jess must have learned directly from the sources. Though I wasn't sure the education was worth feeling ignored. "For real?" I said. "You guys are just going to shoot the shit and chill?"

"Yep. Boys' night out. Get ready. We're leaving in five minutes."

Enticed by the inclusion and convinced there'd be little boozing and posturing, I tossed aside my book, jumped off the couch, and threw on jeans and a hoodie.

We arrived at the only legit all-day, everyday "dyke bar" in the city, or a bar that once seemed like it was strictly for lesbians. Seven years ago, there were no men inside, assuming my memory served me correctly, and perhaps it didn't. I'd just moved to San Francisco from Philadelphia after graduating college a semester early, and as a twenty-one-year-old baby dyke, I needed to pound a few vodka tonics before I could even approach the alley with the neon sign and open those castle doors. By now, I'd convinced myself I belonged. We all did. We all had to when there was only one bar like this in the whole city.

Inside, a handful of men were scattered about—I had no idea whether they were trans or not. I could sometimes feel the undercurrent of tension between the girls and guys over whether the latter were welcome here, but I knew full well I was on the stomping grounds of The Boys, regulars at the place long before they knew trans existed. Tonight, I was afraid I'd have nothing to contribute to their boy banter, be the boring lump on the far side of the gender spectrum where Jess had once placed me, and even the familiar smell of stale beer and sweat socks failed to make me feel at home.

Greg waited for us at a small table near the pinball machine, underneath a provocative photo exhibit. With his black turtleneck sweater and scarf, he had that affected air—European or gay. I figured he was aiming for the second with his fashion when he showed Jess his new gray bandana, decorated with an orgy of un-countable men in unmentionable acts, before returning it to his back left pocket.

A few minutes later, Bec arrived in a dashing white tie and black button-down shirt combo. He had recently shaved his head, as had Jess and Greg. They all looked ready to ship out to boot camp. I wondered if this was intentional, a joint brotherhood thing. Barbershops and military cuts weren't my style. I liked the shaggy skater look, and had let my hair grow into waves that hung down over my eyes and ears.

Jess placed a hand on Bec's shoulder and gave it a squeeze. "You're looking handsome, young man," Jess said.

"Why thank you, sir," Bec replied. He greeted the rest of us before turning to the bar to grab us all drinks. A red hanky stuck out of his back left pocket. The only one with a wallet instead of my color-coded sexual desire sticking out of jeans, I had little inter-est in their uniform accessory or conforming to the dress code of another group.

Bec returned with two Bud Lights in each hand, gripped by their necks, and doled them out before slumping into a seat. I could tell he was tipsy even before his mouth spilled open to pour out brokenhearted anguish. The last to hear about his breakup with Erin, I leaned back in my chair, picking at the label on my beer as the others consoled him.

"You can totally crash at my house. We can cuddle." Greg huddled forward, carelessly blocking me out. He stroked Bec's leg with mock sensuality and said, "If you need me to suck your dick, buddy, I will."

I let out a snort and the front legs of my chair crashed back to the ground with a smack.

"Oh, you think that's funny?" Bec grabbed my hand and placed it on his bulge. He'd said he liked how it looked, but he also liked to gyrate around with it, swiveling his pelvis like a go-go dancer when he broke into his captivating spontaneous dances. "You like?" he said, pressing my hand into his crotch.

Even when Bec teased, he charmed. "Don't you know it," I said, pleased to be involved.

He stared at me from behind glazed eyes, and I held on to see the gears spin, sputter, and stop. "I bet you're the kinkiest one here," he said.

With the right time, place, and girl this might be true, I thought. I tossed him a cocky half smile of acknowledgement and he grabbed his clunky silver belt buckle. In one quick motion, he unlatched it, undid his jeans, and spread his legs. From inside his briefs, he whipped out a realistic looking penis, wiping the smirk off my face. I let out a nervous laugh. I didn't know if he was show-ing me up, expected me to play with it, or if, in his post breakup haze of pain, he was grasping on to it like a security blanket.

With his hand gripped around his packer, he pointed it around, moving with so much control and ease, it seemed at-tached to his body, remarkably so. He gave it a stroke toward Greg. "It's perfect for that blow job. . . ." he teased.

"Or fucking a girl," Jess said, interrupting their ribbing with a tone too aggressive for the lighthearted mood. But it wasn't a conversation about sex until Jess made me want out of the men's locker room.

"Nah. It's a little too soft." Bec razzed Greg with his drunken eyes. "Blow job?"

The idea of a synthetic suck off had sounded ridiculous when

Jess had first mentioned it to me, but there was something both erotic and personal about the way Bec clutched his dick, as if he had a relationship to it, as if it were really truly his. I stared in awe.

"Will you put it away already," Greg demanded.

As Bec effortlessly tucked himself back into his jeans, my shock stayed with me. Where had he learned to wear such a thing, use it, move it, adhere himself to it? With one quick flash, Bec had brought a packer, an inanimate showpiece, to life.

Technically speaking, I had all the working female parts, even knew how to use them to get off. Alone. I obeyed an "If a tree falls in the forest and no one is around to hear it does it make a sound?" philosophy regarding both this individual activity and private area. With my smattering of one- and two-night stands, I'd treated my downstairs as closed for business, unless I'd been slipped enough drinks to let someone sneak in. Lately, I'd been thinking of myself as having a doll crotch, neutered in its construction. Now I wondered if outfitting it with a packer could do more than create a doll with a bulge.

"I think it's that time, gentlemen," Jess said, changing the subject. She brought out the red and yellow cards she'd purchased earlier at a soccer store. "Sorry," she said to me. "I don't have a set for you."

I shrugged my shoulders, not really caring about joining their clubhouse games. I felt like I'd discovered a new toy, a kaleidoscope, endlessly enraptured by the ways The Boys blended, blurred, and reformed the boxes of gender and sexuality, tugging the colored edges into shapes and shades that would never fit onto some linear spectrum.

Used by referees to denote penalties—red for expulsion, yellow for warning—these cards were to be used by this crew as a code to protect against flirting with, dating, or going home with a "crazy" girl. To calibrate their cards, they raised reds and yellows, but mostly reds, to the names of people from their histories. A crazy girl turned out to be someone who stalked your house, sent you to the STD clinic on a false alarm, lived in a shit-hole among mice, or would generally make an awful girlfriend.

"Red flag means step away from the girl," Jess said.

"You can't use a card when you're lonely and want attention."

"You can't use it to cock-block."

"And you need something to back up your call. Concrete information, like she's keyed the car door of an ex."

"Or she's humped someone horrible." Bec flicked his tongue against his red card.

I waited with my hands in my lap, only half listening to their stories about exes and flings and lessons learned. If only someone had saved me, throwing up a red card for Trisha while we slow danced to Prince in the corner of this very bar. A beautiful femme, she spoke about some "friend" all night, which I thought nothing of until she took me home, seduced me, and, about to come, began to scream this "friend's" name. A card protecting me from Sally would've been nice too. During our one sleepover she picked up the phone when her ex-girlfriend called and chatted with her while I lay in her bed—rather harmless but pretty bad form.

As they reminisced, uttering names I barely recognized, I came up with my own matching list to go with theirs—Samantha, Hallie, Kate, Carolyn. I could've come up with something crazy about at least half of them, but as I flashbacked to each experience, there was a unifying theme, one thing they could've thrown at me in the tally, red flagged me right back for: I kept all of my clothes on, I was incapable of physical intimacy, I fucked and fled.

"Can you believe it, guys?" Greg said eventually. "We're all single."

"When was the last time that happened?" Jess asked.

"It's been a long time," Bec acknowledged.

Greg made a fist and held it up over the table. The two others brought their knuckles up to kiss his. "You too, Nina," Bec said, stirring me from my journey though the ghosts of girls past.

I curled my fingers into a ball and brought my fist up to join the triad, but the bump of our hands only solidified how different I felt from them. I was the anomaly, single for the seven years that they were in and out of relationships. They all had something that I did not—some level of sexual comfort with their bodies, some physical connection with others. I glanced at Bec's crotch, could almost feel my hand on his package, except now I envisioned it as mine. On my walk home with Jess, I asked if she'd take me shopping for a packer.

The next morning presented the perfect opportunity. After brunch, a housemate ritual of Jess and Melissa's that I'd passed up too many times for homework, I suggested a postprandial excursion to the nearby Good Vibrations. I was glad to have Melissa with us, considered her a sexual touchstone, a balance of perspective and attitude to ground me around Jess. She also knew about packers, although hers had fallen to the bottom of her toolbox when she moved on from the starter kit.

I was still working, or not working, with a milk crate that held a vibrator, harness, and a half-dozen dildos, all gifts for my twenty-third birthday from a friend who'd worked handcrafting toys at Vixen Creations. With little sex, I had little use for most of my gifts and a store like Good Vibes, but I'd stopped in occasionally, mostly to kill time when meeting people in the neighborhood. Well-lit, tasteful, and expensive, the place reminded me of Whole Foods, except with iridescent purple erections on display.

At the front door, I left my two escorts and followed the beacon of unnaturally vibrant colors to the back wall. I quickly passed over the marbled and glittered dildos, similar to those in my milk crate, and anything that twitched rabbit or dolphin parts. I ignored anything that contained "lady," "fem," or "mermaid" in the name and paused briefly to inspect the realistic bad boys, big guns with names like Bandit and Outlaw. Jess occasionally packed hard with one of these, but she said if there was going to be more than an hour between dinner and "sexy time," the perma-erection would be uncomfortable, not to mention obvious, like popping a Viagra too early. Made for harnesses, the strap-on parts were useless for a bachelor like me.

I picked up a plastic bag holding a Mango Packer, a three-and-a-half-inch dick-like urinating device, and wondered if trans guys really used that kind of thing to stand at the urinal in a men's room. Next to the Mango Packer was something referred to as a "pack 'n' play," a semibendable, half-mast rod similar to the one Bec had whipped out the night before. Still curious as to the kind of "play" it invited, I imagined it should carry a sign like those found at the ski resorts of my youth: Experts Only—Expect Hazards. I figured you needed to be as smooth as Bec to brave the uncertainty and I moved to the end of the line, the beginner-friendly soft packs—just for me, no partner required.

They came in clear boxes with three ice cream flavors as color choices. I couldn't pull off "chocolate." I eliminated the pale "vanilla" for being, well, too vanilla—an unfortunate branding decision by the marketing department—and carried the "caramel" over to Jess and Melissa. I raised the clear box up to my face. Inside, a silicone penis flopped over uneven wrinkly balls. "Does it match my skin color?" I asked with an exaggerated smile.

Melissa laughed louder than Jess, and they both shook their heads dismissively. The fact that the caramel color didn't match my complexion was perhaps inconsequential, since the entire package clashed with my breasts.

"Don't worry, I'll use my library voice next time," I whispered loudly before heading back to the wall.

I found an accessory with a waistband and a single flap of leather, crossed with thin T-shaped elastic bands. Intended to keep the packer in place, it looked like a testicular torture device. Oww, I thought, resisting the urge to cover my crotch with my hand. Then I remembered something Jess said: it didn't matter whether she was packing soft or hard, she felt a connection to these bits (as she called them) like they were her own flesh. I wanted to feel that connection, the weight and heat in my briefs, not some extra barricade of leather against my skin.

To replace her original soft pack, now worn with use, Jess purchased the same VixSkin Mr. Right as me, ignoring my jokes about our matching twinkies. At home, she offered me a black jockstrap to hold mine. "I only wore it once," Jess said. "It's too big for me, but it might fit you."

While I didn't understand how something too big for her could fit me, since we had similarly sized bodies and the same-size dick—five and a half inches including the one-inch base, which I'd heard was cheating to count—I considered "once" like the "five-second rule" for salvaging dropped food and happily took the jockstrap off her hands.

I flipped it around, looking for an opening. "Where do you put the cup?" I asked.

"It's a gay boy jockstrap. For arranging your package."

"Oh," I said, disappointed that my new jockstrap wasn't white, smelly, and made for protection during sports.

In my room, I arranged myself in the jockstrap and put my jeans on over it. I opened my door to the long hallway where both Melissa and Jess waited. I felt exposed without underwear. "Can I wear my boxers over the jockstrap?" I asked. "Or is it wrong to cover it up with three layers and a sweater?"

"I like to pack in briefs," Jess said.

I thought of her silk leopard-spotted briefs, the ironic '70s porn-star style, and her more serious, pink metrosexual manties—neither of which I'd ever attempt. I stepped toward Melissa, imploring her with my eyes.

"I haven't packed in years. But boxer briefs work too," Melissa said. "*You* can do whatever *you* want."

"Packing does take some getting used to," Jess added.

They followed me into the living room, where I checked both my front and side view in the mirror. Facing forward, I grabbed my crotch and readjusted my bulge. Goddamn, I look good, I thought. But unlike my first binder sighting, I wasn't compelled to blurt out this self-congratulation. I was no longer shocked that a reflection of myself presenting dude-like anatomy made me feel attractive. Seeing my flat chest along with my package elicited a quiet euphoria. "I like it already," I said.

For the rest of the afternoon, while hanging out at my house, I kept my soft pack in the contour pouch of my tightest pair of boxer briefs, trying to get used to moving around with it. When I walked, it slipped to various locations around my pelvic area, and each time I sat down, it rose up in a slightly different location, like a mole, or maybe like a dick. There was no denying it was odd to have an artificial object resting loosely in my underwear, but the weight I'd anticipated replaced a visceral emptiness that seemed more tangible now that it had been filled. Where there had been nothing before, there was now something. The dead zone of my doll crotch had been awakened. I had substance. Junk that I wanted to see and touch.

In front of my own private mirror, I checked myself out as if it was my job and my job was modeling like Marky Mark. With the button of my jeans open and the fly unzipped and teasing, I offered my shy boy-next-door smile; with both hands cupped around my stuff, I gave my modest, caught naked look; in silliness, I briefly pulled the dick part over the top of my underwear as if I might pee; for a while I just kept grabbing my package and making badass faces. It was liberating to finally have a private part I wanted to engage with and get to know. We even sat on the couch and read together. It didn't matter that nobody else saw us, or that the mirrors had been put away. The simple awareness of what was in my pants made me feel secure and happy.

When I saw Jess in the kitchen later that night, I was so excited about connecting with my packer, I had to share. "Guess what," I said. "I'm still wearing my penis."

She wagged her head disapprovingly. "It's not a penis," she said with the same hard edge she reserved for talking about men.

"Okay," I said, figuring I must have offended her with my correlation to the group she detested. "Then what is it?"

"It's a *cock*," she said. "We're tough."

I felt scolded and confused. "But the packer doesn't do anything."

"Then you can call it a softie."

I didn't want a *cock*, a word that signified much of what I despised in men, and occasionally in Jess: cockiness, superiority, egotism. For the first time that day, I wondered if I was doing something catastrophic by appropriating a body part that didn't belong to me if along with it came an attitude of power, control, and arrogance.

I couldn't wait for a social event, a reason to pack in public. The first opportunity came the following week, an A-gay holiday happy hour at their local neighborhood hangout. A monthly visitor to their circle ever since grad school started, I'd been steadily losing interest in them as a group, only to have it dissolve completely after the pool party a couple months earlier. Had I not been on school break and eager to show off the new me in my pants, I probably would've stayed home.

I heard Tori immediately. Her brazen holler greeted me as I stepped through the front entrance. She'd make the perfect test case, I thought. She wasn't a man-hater, and she wouldn't accuse me of falling for self-loathing dick replacement—I'd seen *The Vagina Monologues* too many times for that. There was always the risk she'd say something offensive, but that only spared me the worry over offending or alarming her. I chatted her up about work, life, nothing at all, really, just waiting until she noticed. I kept a few feet between us, giving her eyes the opportunity to roam below my waist. I even brushed my hand against my fly a few times, hoping to draw her attention there. Finally, I grew impatient and placed her hand on my bulge.

She flinched and her jaw nearly hit her chest. "Are you . . . ? Is that . . . ?"

"Packing," I said, nodding.

"That's quite a . . ." She did an about-face and gripped the bar with both hands. "Wow," she said, before turning back to me.

"Cool, huh?"

"I had a friend, a drag performer, with one of those, what do you call them, packers?" she said. Tori began to ramble about this friend and I pretended to listen while my frustration grew. I wasn't packing for a show. I wanted her to acknowledge, validate, or congratulate me on my man stuff, or at the very least, ask something that pertained to me.

"You want a beer?" she offered finally.

I held up my half-full Budweiser. "You just got me one." We stood there silent and awkward as the chasm expanded. An eternity passed before a few friends, including my boss Beth, delivered a telegram from Zippy—my presence was requested on the back patio.

"Zippy's here?" I asked. "For real?"

"Surprise!" Beth said.

For a brief moment, I was sad that Zippy hadn't told me about her visit. But then I realized Christmas was approaching and I also hadn't bothered to call her to see when she'd be arriving into town. Neither of us would make a big deal about it, which is why our friendship worked. And if there was one person who'd play along, interested in all my experiences and observations, it would be Zippy.

I speed walked outside, spotted her alone in the corner of the courtyard, and put my head down to avoid the pod of smokers and the requisite round of "What's up, lady?" hellos. I marched directly up to the wooden bench where Zippy sat, let her "Hey, girl" shoot directly through my ears, and before she could rise to greet me, I jammed my bulging crotch toward her eye level. I turned in profile and then forward. "Do you notice anything different about me?"

"Goo!" she said, rising. "Either you have a sock in your pants, or you're happy to see me."

"Of course I'm happy to see you." I hugged her, throwing in a friendly grinding hump.

"Oh, baby, oh baby," she cried. "That ain't no sock."

I told her exactly what I had in my pants, everything about the size, shape, color, price, shopping excursion. Her amped-up energy only heightened my enthusiasm. She clapped her hands together. "I wanna see. I wanna see," she said.

I wrapped her hand in mine and pulled her across the stone courtyard, away from the men at the picnic table, and into an empty corner behind the unused patio bar. I shot a quick glance over my shoulder, as if I were about to display a selection of dime bags, and reached down into my jeans without opening them. I removed my packer from my boxer briefs and held it low, cupped in my hand.

Her eyes expanded like flowers blooming in time lapse. "Coooool," she said, reaching out with her fingers.

I pulled the packer away from her. "Do you really want to touch that?"

Zippy put her hands behind her back and interlocked her fingers to prevent an accident. She leaned her head in for closer inspection. "It looks so real."

"It's too big to be real," I said proudly. I gave her a few seconds to stare uninterrupted and then looked over my shoulder again before returning the packer to its home. I tucked it underneath slightly, so it wasn't overly conspicuous.

"Did you name it?" Zippy asked.

"Name it? What are you talking about?"

"All guys name their ding-dongs."

I pondered this and then decided she was wrong.

"I bet your brother has a name for his," she said. "Call him."

Even if some boys did name theirs, I figured it was those macho types, insecure about their masculinity, not my brother. The kid was tough all right, especially in sports like ice hockey, but he was the kind of guy who proved himself with assists first and goals second, never fists and dick. I pushed "Bro" on my phone and he picked up with an animated hello.

"I'm sorry. I can't really talk," I apologized. "But I need to ask you something. Do you have a name for your, um, ding-dong?"

"No, of course not," he said.

"Are you sure?" I asked. "Like maybe when you were a kid?"

My brother was almost four years younger than me, and he didn't ask door-opening questions. He knew that I wore men's underwear, and that when I asked him whether my latest hair-cut made me appear boyish, the best reply was, "Do you want to look boyish?" Even when I answered yes he didn't press the issue. He thought I lived on a lesbian planet so different from the one on which he lived that more information without a spaceship and translator would be of no use. Little did he know that I was on a puddle jumper to a smaller, yet queerer place.

"Dude, I just don't refer to it," he said.

"Do other guys name them?"

My brother asked the guys watching football with him if they had names for theirs. I couldn't hear over the sportscaster in the background how he'd phrased the question, what words he'd used, but no one admitted to a name.

"Call his girlfriend," Zippy said after I hung up. "I bet she has a name for it."

Although I contemplated calling his girlfriend, we would have to catch up before I could ask her, and I'd lost interest.

Even if she and my brother had a pet name, he didn't need a name to bring his dick to life, same as he didn't need to whip it out in a bar to prove to a friend that it existed. He didn't need accessories or language to make himself known. I was not and would not ever be a boy like him. Although now that the area around my balls itched, I felt like a jerk for all those times I yelled at him to stop adjusting himself in front of the TV, especially when I tattled to our mother.

And I was beginning to think that I now shared a responsibility with him. With my packer, my awareness burgeoned with the complications and consequences of relating to a body part symbolic of so much more than anatomy. I told Zippy about the "penis" reprimand I'd received from Jess, how uncomfortable I'd felt when Jess had banged out the word *cock*.

"Come on," Zippy said. "The only place you can ever use the word *penis* is in a doctor's office. Is this why you don't get laid? Would you ever tell a chick she has a hot vagina?"

Zippy had a point. "You know, the last time a guy offered to show me his cock, I gave him a blow job." I continued to speak through her giggles. Talking about boys and sex was one of our favorite pastimes.

"I just don't want to be some douche-bag guy," I said. "And sometimes Jess comes off like that to me." For all her talk about not wanting to be a man, it had to be their privilege that made her bitter, because to me, she talked about sex like the dominating, callous men I wanted nothing to do with.

Zippy told me a story about being at the dyke bar a couple years ago. Jess was playing pool and, trying to line up her next shot, she ended up near a small crowd that included Zippy's girlfriend. "Jess leaned into her and he was all," Zippy dropped into a mock deep voice, " 'Excuse me, is my *stick* in your way?' "

I was shocked to hear Zippy use the male pronoun for someone who wasn't in the process of a transition. This was so outside her realm of understanding, it had to be an insult. "He?" I asked.

"*He* sounded like a male pig," Zippy said. "Being a dyke doesn't mean you can act like a prick."

Actually, in Jess's world, I was starting to think it did. The very reason Jess kept female pronouns around was to avoid direct association with men, so that she'd be a subversive queer with a stick, an equal to women, rather than a dude with a dick, the entitled enemy. To me they were one and the same when delivering macho pickup lines, which I found obnoxious regardless of gender. But that was Jess's job as my older brother, to test out the boundaries for us both. She had given me her jockstrap; she was family, and I didn't like the way Zippy was talking about her.

"What if Jess just wanted to go home with someone who liked the pole, not the hole?" I argued.

"Aren't there better ways to express that?" Zippy said.

Jess's sexual energy often frustrated me, and I did wonder whether, if she could stop resenting men so much, she would accept herself a bit more, the guy parts she clearly identified with, and stop acting out their insecurities. But I also wondered if I was projecting all my own ingrained perceptions and personal issues on to Jess, because as much as it surprised me, as much as I couldn't quite wrap my head around it, some women loved her commanding, direct approach, considered it the essence of being secure. Our attitudes were so different, Jess and I; she was assertive where I was self-deprecating, and although I'd go to extremes to avoid replicating behavior that I associated with jerk guys, like using a pool cue like a phallus, I did want my body to represent the way I saw it. When it came to how we understood our bodies, Jess and I were similar.

"It's not easy to express," I said to Zippy. "When you tease me about hitting on straight girls, you assume I have a hooha. And that's not the way I see it." I told her, as well as I could, how my packer had shifted my physical sense of self, acted as a vehicle to visualize myself with male parts and allowed me to actually relate to my body below the belt. For me, there definitely was a connection between attitude and anatomy, but instead of having a dick turning me into a dick, it made me feel comfortable and at peace.

As Zippy listened intently, I imagined this conversation was one of the better ways, but I couldn't explain my body one by one to everyone. Wearing a packer was another way to express myself, and yet I'd shoved it at Tori so that she would notice, nearly begging her to see me in a new light. For as much as I wanted to indict some trans guys when I caught what sounded like misogyny, I could often see both sides of the rift I noticed inside queer spaces—strong, confident women pissed about former dykes turning into asshole dudes and these very guys referring to these women as transphobic for refusing to acknowledge, accept, or respect their new identities.

Zippy and I talked uninterrupted, challenging each other and laughing until we were exhausted, like old times. The next day, she left a message on my voice mail. "I just called to say thank you for showing me your cock last night." I saved the message. And I continued to resave it every thirty days. Zippy never greeted me with "Hey, girl" again.

Six

WINGS

On a Tuesday morning in early January, at eleven o'clock on the dot, I marched up the long, narrow staircase to Greg's apartment. At the top, I stopped and patted my pockets, the contents the ostensible purpose of my visit. I made out the hard shield of my notebook, as well as my pen, backup pen, and backup to the backup pen. I knocked on the front door, a journalist reporting on Greg's first testosterone shot.

For most of my winter break, I'd read voraciously, covering more than a thousand pages of transgender history, science, memoir, and narrative nonfiction books, as well as various legal, medical, psychological, and archived documents—literally anything I could find through the internet or library. The worst were the third-person narratives, written by journalists who treated their subjects like zoo animals. I thought I could better, I needed some new material for my upcoming semester, and so, when I bumped into Greg at my house on his way to the gym, I asked if I could observe and write about him.

"What are you going to write, 'Greg the Trans Guy' is on the elliptical machine?" he mocked.

So much for doing better, I thought. I wanted to write about "Greg the Person," the deceptively sweet, hilarious guy who'd probably crack some killer jokes on the elliptical machine. But it was true that personally, I wanted to know about "Greg the Trans Guy," and after my night out with The Boys a few weeks before, I couldn't see this happening organically. Greg and I had settled into the area between acquaintances and friends, a place filled with enough care that I felt horrible for offending him.

I apologized immediately, but before I could even finish, excitement overcame him. "Forget about it," he said. "You should come over tomorrow at eleven—I'm getting my first T-shot!"

The next day, Greg opened his front door to the apartment he shared with at least a few others. A long hallway with a handful of doors stretched the length of the floor. I followed him directly into his room, cramped with mismatched furniture and, with only one cloistered window, devoid of natural light. In the corner, a TV—a loaner from his surgery recovery—rested on a table, and in front sat a folding chair for visitors. His room had that warm, lived-in feel, as if he'd holed up in there for a while.

Greg handed me his prescription for testosterone cypionate and took off padding around the house. I deciphered the scribble, which called for biweekly intramuscular injections ramping up to 200 mg, a "standard" dose for a trans man. Greg's tube socks swished past the carpeted doorway several times before he reentered. "Check this out," he said, handing me a two-page printout.

I read the top, "A Letter to Would-Be Transsexuals," by the American Boyz, a support organization for FTMs, female-to-male transsexuals. Greg paced in semicircles around his bed while I uncovered the potential pitfalls of "sex reassignment." The summarized version went like this: You will be discriminated against; finding employment might be difficult; you won't ever have a "normal" body of the opposite sex; naked, you will be an education campaign and potentially a freak show; your dating pool will shrink; you may lose your friends and family; adopting children will be difficult; there are certain countries you can never visit; you will be dependent on a substance created by large corrupt pharmaceutical companies; statistically, you are more likely to be killed by hatemongers; and people will ask you about your genitalia . . . *for the rest of your life.*

"What a buzz kill," Greg said when I was done. "My therapist gave that to me last night."

The list functioned as a know-before-you-go to transsexual country, a warning like the "dangers and annoyances" section of a *Lonely Planet* guidebook, a few paragraphs that would always scare me even when traveling to a relatively safe place like the Netherlands. "Probably not the kind of stuff you want to think about right now," I said. I'd been at his house for five minutes and could already tell that I was too invested in his well-being to keep a reporter's objective distance.

Greg told me that he was taking testosterone in order to *pass*, the word many trans guys used for being recognized as men despite the term's complex and colorful history. Greg wanted to see and hear the man that he was, and he wanted his identity acknowledged and reflected by others. For him, his decision to start testosterone was straightforward.

The handout served as a gut check, one final reconciliation. Had I any interest in passing, I probably would've still turned back at number two, "discrimination," never making it anywhere near number twenty, and certainly not to the last sentence in the handout, the welcome sign that read: "You can be yourself here, but you'd better learn quickly how to survive."

I looked up to see a young man materialize in the bedroom doorway. He wore a mesh ball cap, a five o'clock shadow, and hollow expanders in his ears. Removing his leather jacket, his forearms flashed like the flanks of a Thunderbird, streaked with dark ink and fiery stars. He embraced Greg with a couple hearty thumps to the back. He turned to me. "I'm Jack," he said. The hoop piercing his lip curled up into a sexy smile.

I almost swooned. "Nina," I finally forced out.

He gripped my hand in a firm shake. I quickly explained that I was in a writing program, working on some trans-themed stories, and asked his permission to take notes. He told me his last experience with a journalist had been negative, the angle of the final piece bothered him, and yet he was unconcerned by my presence. "Take notes or whatevs," he said. "Do what you need to do."

I was pretty sure he'd just given me permission to mess up,

something I now considered a foregone conclusion. Because to me, Jack was completely new, a walking education campaign, everything about him intriguing. And he probably thought of himself as just a guy, a person who ate, breathed, and pissed like the rest of us—wait, how did he piss, sitting or standing up? No wonder he'd acted aloof—dealing with people like me all the time must suck.

I moved out of their way, trying not to block the dim light coming in through the window, and sat in the folding chair next to the bookcase. I jotted down a few titles—*Middlesex, In a Queer Time and Place,* and *Stupid White Men*—figuring a good journalist would stop admiring Jack's emo-boy skater style and take some notes.

From under his bed, Greg removed a Tupperware box holding a vial and prepackaged needles and handed it to Jack. "Is there any way to stop the zits?" Greg asked.

"You can go to a dermatologist," Jack replied, slipping on a pair of black latex gloves and unwrapping the packaging on the needles.

"How long does it last?"

"Going on four years for me."

Jack filled up the syringe, talking Greg through the preparation process. Eventually Greg would need to learn to do his shots himself if he wanted to continue with testosterone for the long term, which would be necessary to maintain some of the effects, but, scared of needles, he'd sought the help of his friend. Greg situated himself, placing his hands on the Oakland Raiders blanket on the back of his bed. He stepped one foot forward into a lunge.

"Put weight on your left leg," Jack said, standing behind him. "My practice may seem strange, but I'm gonna spank you. It'll loosen you up, make it hurt less."

Greg turned his head around. "I'm all for spanking, but really?"

"Trust me." Jack pulled Greg's T-shirt up and slapped him five times above the waistband of his Fruit of the Loom underwear.

I shifted in my seat, reminding myself to breathe. I hated

needles. The sight of them nearly made me pass out. I'd learned to look away during my own vaccination shots and to focus on something concrete. I liked numbers and found math exercises as calming as counting sheep. There were 365 days in a year, 52 weeks, and 26 shot cycles. In four years, Jack had stuck himself 104 times. In the next twenty years, Greg would have to do this, five hundred something . . . I inhaled deeply. I promised myself I wouldn't look away.

Jack grabbed a wedge of flesh, just above Greg's ass, and held it between his thumb and index finger. Using his other hand, he stuck the needle into the muscle, slowly emptying the syringe. He extracted the needle and covered the site with a pink Hello Kitty Band-Aid. I exhaled.

"Is that it?" Greg asked.

"I told you. I fucking rule," Jack said.

Greg opened his arms and enveloped Jack in a warm bear hug. "I didn't feel anything. Thank you."

I noticed the high pitch of Greg's voice for the first time. How soon that would change. Everything would. I could recite all of the expected changes from the definitive *Medical Therapy and Health Maintenance for Transgender Men: A Guide for Health Care Providers*. The permanent and reversible effects mingled in a dissonant clinical poem: heightened sex drive, muscle growth, fat redistribution, increased body odor, facial and body hair growth, clit growth, stretching of the vocal chords, weight gain. With that shot, Greg had triggered male puberty. If he continued his biweekly injections, he'd break through the squeaky voice and adolescent acne into adulthood and be rewarded with the traits common among grown men, like male pattern balding.

It was hard to tell which were the desired effects and which the side effects. The clinical poem sounded like the FDA-required warnings on prescription drug commercials where I found myself asking if anyone would really "ask your doctor" about the latest and greatest drug if "thoughts of suicide" and "anal leakage" were mentioned as possible outcomes. But the cold detached language of medicine had a way of fading into the warm flesh and blood of the actual people who benefited from the treatment.

Greg placed the covered needles and vial back into the Tupperware box and sat cross-legged on his bed. "Do you remember what your first shot felt like?" he asked Jack.

"It's changed over the years. Now it's like nothing to me," Jack said. He was perched awkwardly on the edge of the bed. On a silver chain around his neck, I noticed the Hebrew characters for *L'Chaim,* meaning "to life." As he'd tell me later, he got the chain after his eighteenth birthday, around the time he began taking testosterone.

Starting hormones had been the first step in Jack's transition, before having the more expensive top surgery—the common path among FTMs. I'd recently discovered from my books that the term *transgender* was initially created by gender benders with no desire for surgery or hormones who wanted to separate themselves from *transsexuals,* those who desired to legally and medically change their sex. But now *transgender* acted as a uniting umbrella term for all nonnormative genders, and for Jack's generation, *trans* seemed to be the shorthand for everything. He was twenty-two and a decade younger than Greg, but his experience elevated him to elder in the room.

"When is stuff gonna start happening?" Greg ducked his head, leaned forward, and whispered. "Like my hooha?"

"Oh, you'll feel it," Jack said. "You'll be like, whoa, hi. You may be creeped out at first. But the tranny cock is fun."

I added *tranny cock* to my list of names for the *dicklet,* or what those reliant on textbook physiology called an enlarged clit.

"Can you penetrate with it?" Greg asked expectantly.

"Kinda. If you find the right angle," Jack said. "Trust me. It's worth it. The teeny weeny changes *everything.*"

I wrote down *teeny weeny,* wondering if it was something I could, in good conscience, publish. I had quickly learned rule number one in transgender etiquette was not to focus or define people by what's between their legs; this made sense—in daily life, I paid no attention to the genitals of cisgender—or "cis"—people, as my readings referred to folks who are not trans, those with gender identities and presentations that "match" the sex they were assigned at birth. But nowhere in the medical literature or the personal stories I'd read did anyone mention "waking up with morning wood" as Jack just did, nor make it sound so appealing.

Like me, Greg understood what T did in theory, but he wanted to know what it had done to Jack, and by extension what it would do to him. "Does your orgasm change?" Greg asked.

"I used to have more. Now one and I'm done for a while," Jack said. "But it's big."

"Are you less emotional?"

"I'm less labile. But I'm still emo."

"Can you cry?"

"I don't cry often."

"Is that bad?"

"Sometimes I feel like I need to, but I can't."

"We should get you *Beaches* or *Steel Magnolias*. Or maybe a guy movie, like *Rudy*."

Greg fired away relentlessly, asking over and over again about emotions, acne, shaving, joint pain, spatial sense, smell, taste, energy levels. The effects were too enormous to contemplate. I understood having a physical sense of self in the male ballpark, especially now that I'd experimented with packing, but to live as a man seemed so extreme. Unbearably uncertain. How did Greg know that after devoting the next couple years to a second puberty and a life-altering change that he would be happy to be recognized and treated as a man? I flicked my pen against the side of my chair in anticipation of each question.

"Do bowel movements change?" Greg asked.

"Uh-huh. Because of the oil. More times a day, not solid."

"So, it's true. Men are full of shit," Greg said. "Will I not want to cuddle? Will I stop asking for directions?"

A guffaw shot out of my mouth.

Jack turned around to face me. "Aren't you supposed to be taking notes?"

I looked down at my blank piece of paper, my pen frozen in my hand. Embarrassed, I tipped my notebook up toward me.

"Oh, I'm just teasing ya," Jack said. His mouth curved up into that charming moon sliver of a smile. Had I believed I was anything more than a naïve little pest, I might've engaged with my own coy reply. "I'm catching a few things," I said instead, and jotted down: *Are you any different from them?* My mind had run off on a marathon of what testosterone could do to me. *Would you be happier as a man?* I wrote, and closed my notebook.

If I wanted to be a man, I would know, I thought. I would have to know. I would always have known. Wasn't that what my trans reading course was teaching me, what Greg had been trying to tell me with his stories of stuffing his underwear with a sock as a kid, his recollections of peeing standing up?

Greg tapped Jack on the leg. "Hey, what are you doing now? You want to go to Hooters?"

"Fuck yeah," Jack sang.

"Are you guys serious?" I asked.

"The wings are to die for," Greg said.

I found chains and greasy food awful enough without throwing the exploitation of women's bodies into the mix. I knew the argument that a woman could choose whether to work at Hooters or not, but until there were as many "schlongstaurants" run by women as there were "breastaurants" run by men, I wasn't buying it. Greg and Jack didn't so much invite me as they didn't care one way or another if I tagged along, and I returned to my reporter role to avoid my moral quandary about patronizing Hooters.

The bright light of the sun did little to cut the crisp winter chill. A brisk wind blew debris, leaves, and trash along the sidewalk. The two of them walked stride for stride and I trailed behind, allowing them a respite from the interloping journalist. Greg threw his arm around Jack and pulled him in close, knocking his cap off in an affectionate headlock. With that one move, Greg shattered the last of my doubt that underneath his hard shell there was anything but a tender heart.

At his shiny blue Hyundai, Jack opened the passenger side door and I climbed into the backseat. Within seconds, Greg launched another inquisition, this one about body hair growth. "Do you get hair on your upper legs?" Greg asked.

Driving down a deserted side street, Jack kept one hand on the wheel and used the other to unlatch the silver skeleton buckle on his belt. He untucked his white undershirt from his jeans. "Sorry," he said in my direction.

Uncertain whether Jack was referring to the prospective peep show or his loss of driving control as the car wobbled across the whole street, I pushed myself forward between the seats. "Oh, it's fine," I said. "I want to see."

Jack slowed down the car, tapped the steering wheel once with his palm to keep us from veering off into the line of parked cars, and then lifted his ass to scootch down his jeans. Ignoring the road, the three of us focused on the same spot as if searching for gold. We found only a pale upper thigh with thick black hair. "You won't have as much hair as me," Jack said to Greg. "I'm a Russian Jew."

I too was part Russian Jew, other parts Ukrainian, Polish, and uncertain other hair-producing Eastern European countries. I blamed my genealogy for the dog names the boys in elementary school had taunted me with, the leg-shaving intervention by my bunkmates at sleepaway camp, and the brow waxing my first girl-friend demanded to shape the thick strips over my eyes. I clipped my seatbelt back across my lap and stared out the window. The thought of being a hairy man with back felt, ear whiskers, and butt fuzz made me queasy.

Using the back of his hand, Greg stroked Jack's bristly cheek. "You really are a hairy beast," he said.

"Aww, thanks, man," Jack said, tilting his head away with a coquettish smile.

Inside the restaurant, we found a table surrounded by couples, tourists, families with young children, and, closest to us, a group of fraternity boys who hadn't learned the rule that Greek lettering should not be visible on more than one article of clothing. Our waitress's tits approached us, shooting out of owl eyes. The rest of her body, clad in orange lycra running shorts that provided less coverage than my underwear, followed. Even her bunchy white leggings stretched over fake-tan panty hose couldn't make me smile. The play on the archetypal cheerleader was too close to reality to be funny.

After our waitress took our orders, Greg brought up his fear that the T-fueled sex drive would consume him.

"It'll get bad," Jack said. "You just have to find time to whack it."

"What if I ogle bodies all the time?" Greg said. "That's not me."

Off to the side of us, our waitress clipped our order ticket to a caliper and shot it down a string to the kitchen. Her tits jiggled long after the ticket was gone. Neither of my companions noticed.

"I objectify guys, but not girls," Jack said.

They slipped into a discussion about hooking up with men after starting testosterone, a somewhat common outcome. In Jack's case, he said his attraction to men had to do with his increased horniness, but also his newfound ability to act on his interest once others saw him as a man.

As Jack schooled Greg on hooking up with men, both cisgender and transgender, I was blown away by his experiences, that he would fuck a man in a gay sex club, using but not disclosing his strap-on. His confidence was riveting, his sexuality fascinating. He dated the whole panorama of genders, he said; *pansexual* was the word he used. There was even space for me within the vast genderscape of his interests. I imagined that Jack, who once had a female body like mine, could lift the hood on this hybrid, see that inside I ran on a bit of something else.

Listening to Jack speak so boldly, I could tell he was one of

those special charismatically self-assured people that others
would make an exception to be with—older women dating below
their age cutoff, cis guys sleeping with their first trans guy, dykes
discovering their interest in men. I was certainly ready to revise
my rules of attraction for him, or maybe Jack, sexy even with
orange-tinted grease on his face, sparked what I already knew: I
liked men.

As I watched the two of them become absorbed in the pile of
wings, my entire sexual history suddenly started coming together
in my head. Despite my prior efforts to fit in with my A-gays, I
wasn't exclusively interested in women like they were. Screw Tori,
Stephanie, and all the rest of them who said, "Give it a rest, you big
dyke," every time I spoke of a crush on a dude. No wonder I liked
to give guys head—that was the only way to act on my desire while
distracting all attention away from my body. The problem was my
body. I had the self-image of a guy—flat chest, no hips, muscles, a
dick. But inside Hooters, there was nothing I wanted less than to
be grouped together with the whole lot of them.

In front of me a display advertised a glossy pinup calendar
for customers to purchase for the soldiers in Iraq. I imagined it,
too, was part of the campy aesthetic, a throwback to World War II
and Vietnam soldiers with postcards of naked chicks as their sole
source of female contact. The thought of guys killing each other
and turning to Hooters girls as jerk-off fodder reinforced stereo-
types that made me sicker than the wings. I stopped even picking
at my food and counted down the minutes until I could get out
of there.

After lunch, Jack offered to drive me back to work. We left Greg
at the Wharf and continued on the path alongside a strip of urban
sand pretending to be a beach. Walking in silence, the inequality
of the day's exchange weighed on me. Having kept quiet, attempting and pretty much failing to be an objective reporter, my need
to connect overcame me. "You know how I'm writing about trans

issues," I said. My eyes followed the swim lanes, ropes extending out into the frigid waters only brave souls dared to enter. "Well, some of my interest is personal."

Jack twisted his head up. "I know. It always is."

I fought the urge to return his smile, hoping to hide my crush. I focused on the choppy white caps of the ocean, the outcropping of stone rising into the island of Alcatraz. "How did you make the decision to transition?" I asked. "At such a young age?"

As we climbed the short hill to his car, he told me about his teenage years, the whirlwind tour of sexual identities—bisexual, then dyke, then queer. He'd been a queer youth activist, and at a leadership training retreat, both the presence of a trans kid and a lesson on the difference between sex and gender (or biology and cultural sense of self, as they are often defined) triggered him. "I knew I wasn't a woman. I didn't know what I was, but I knew I wasn't a woman." He turned his key in the passenger door. "I was scared to death."

I felt my own fear rising as he spoke, too similar was my own self-realization. For as much as I tried to believe I could want a flat chest without also wanting to live as a man, that top surgery and hormones were separate decisions with extremely different physical, social, medical, and financial impacts, what if they were more closely linked than I thought? What if on the other side of *not woman* there was only one other option: *man?* What if the rest of the panorama were just words, the middle ground a place most people couldn't see?

Jack drove down the main thoroughfare of Van Ness, the only street in the city that reminded me of a suburban strip mall with its chain stores, chain restaurants, and a multiplex movie theater. The traffic was thick, start and stop every few lights. Jack continued to talk, explaining that he eventually grew tired of the "mindfuck" of seeing his female body in the mirror. Instinct drove his decision to physically transition and hindsight solidified his certainty.

Then Jack recounted an anecdote from his childhood as if it had been told hundreds of times, as if it were legend. As a five-year-old girl, Jack had run around the playground at school shouting, "I'm a boy, I'm a boy." Another kid, trying to be helpful, told him that he could have a "sex-change operation" when he grew up. So, later that afternoon, over Doritos and a peanut butter and jelly sandwich, Jack said to his social worker parents, "Guess what I'm going to do when I grow up? I'm going to have a sex-change operation."

He shared this story like it was his origin tale—it seemed like every trans person had one—evidence that he always knew he was a man. "You can't escape who you are," Jack said as he switched lanes and sped through a yellow light.

I racked my brain, ransacking my childhood in search of a moment when I'd claimed myself as a boy, only to be shut down and told never to mention it again. Maybe I'd been too scared to make such a grand statement to my parents. By the time I was twelve, I was already so afraid of my father that instead of telling him I wanted to stop competing in tennis, I pretended to attend my lessons for almost a year, sometimes waiting out the last ten minutes in our apartment building's laundry room so as not to arrive home early and arouse suspicion.

I followed my past through my teenage years and tried to remember if I was unhappy, fundamentally so. The answer was no. I hated dresses and wearing girly clothes, and having some type of adolescent sexual awakening beyond blow jobs in bathrooms would've been nice, but I enjoyed high school as much as anyone. To the best of my recollections, being a girl wasn't anything I'd ever questioned for nearly thirty years.

I expected to feel relief. If the proof that a person was transgender came in the form of the long-sustained narrative, the history of always knowing, then I was in the clear. I wouldn't have to worry about knives, needles, discrimination, ostracism, acne, losing my job, friends, family, none of it. Yeah, I felt much better about myself when I was binding and packing, but I hadn't been fighting my whole life against some Great Truth. I should have felt relief.

Our car lurched as we stopped short at a red light, and I jerked forward. My seatbelt dug into my chest. "Sorry about that," Jack said.

At Market Street, I suggested I take public transportation the rest of the way rather than have him drive into the heart of downtown. It would be quicker, easier, less painful for us both. In the Mid-Market abyss, a stretch that served mostly as a link between heavily populated areas, he pulled over. "Not everyone gets up and faces their fears every day. I do. And I'm stronger because of it," Jack said, just before I jumped out of the car. I slammed the door shut, but his words stayed with me.

"I lied to skip work and went to Hooters today," I blurted out the second Jess walked into the kitchen.

Lately, our hellos moved so quickly from binding discussions to sir/ma'am moments to gossip about the transitional decisions of others that the "hello" no longer seemed necessary.

"Have you ever been to Hooters with Greg?" I asked. "He claims the wings are to die for. I don't even eat wings." I took a big bite of my sautéed kale, tofu, and rice.

"There are plenty of other places to eat hot wings." Jess pulled a burrito out of a brown paper bag and placed it on a plate. He threw his jacket and beanie on the living room chair before hopping up onto the corner of the tiled counter.

Immediately after my conversation with Zippy, I'd made the switch to male pronouns for Jess. I asked his permission, aware that my use of language could push him too far into man land, but I also told him that when I saw him, it felt right to refer to him as "he." With that one comment, his entire marble facade cracked into pure pride, and I felt the satisfaction of finally recognizing what he needed and trumping the rules that had once stood in my way to offer it to him.

"Would you ever go to Hooters?" I moved the olive oil and salt to the edge of the wooden table next to the stove and sat down.

"No." He crunched on a chip.

"Not even with trans guys?" I asked. "They flirted and gayed out the whole time, spent the entire meal objectifying men, talking about how much easier it is to mess around with dudes once you start passing. Isn't there a 'get out of PC jail free' card for trans-fagging it up in Hooters?"

"Nope." Jess crunched on another chip. "We all choose what we support by where we spend our money. And I will never support Hooters."

I put my bowl down and ran my hand over the finished surface of the table that Jess had spent a week sanding and refinishing in the basement. The work had given him tiny calluses on his hands that we called *manjuries,* a word used sarcastically to refer to any injury sustained doing a "man's work."

"I just don't get it," Jess said. "How do you give up woman to become man and then go to Hooters?"

I considered the irony of Jack holding the one-year anniversary of his top surgery there, taking a commemorative photo with a couple waitresses. "The more I read, the more I hear . . ." I started. "I don't think those guys, I don't think any trans guy ever considered himself a woman."

"Look, I thought I was a boy as a child, too," Jess said. "But it's too easy to say, 'I've always been this way, I'm always going to be this way, so I'm going to transition.' There has to be something new. And maybe this is the old-school lesbian feminist in me, but I feel a responsibility to support the sisterhood, to not assume the privileges that are denied to women." Jess's voice rose before he stopped and shook his head. "You know how I feel about male privilege. Do you really want to hear me go off?"

I shook my head no. It's not that I didn't agree with Jess, but more and more his rant made me defensive, as if he was attacking the part of me that felt connected to men. "Look, I will never go to Hooters again," I said. "But that doesn't change the fact that there's not one thing about me or my body that I consider of or relating to *woman*." I started to kick my legs underneath me in frustration, pumping as if on a swing. "Not one itty-bitty minor thing. When I interact with a girl, I consider it a purely heterosexual interaction. And," I added, rising on the power of finally owning my attraction to dudes, "when I think about men, it's in the gay way!"

"I get it," Jess said. "My interactions with girls are heterosexual, too. But I don't want to be a heterosexual man."

"And I get that," I said. But there was no greater conundrum. How could he, how could I, truly embody heterosexual relationships with women and not take on at least some of the traits associated with men? And then what, I'd be seen as part of the group responsible for breastaurants? "I'm starting to get lost," I said. "I have no idea what's right and wrong anymore." I grasped on to the only thing I was starting to be sure about. "When I think of myself physically," I said, "I am a man."

"Me, too," he said. "But politically, I am a woman."

"What does that mean?" I begged.

He jumped off the counter. "It means fighting for equality of the sexes. Equal pay. Equal space. Equal everything. Across the board, women make less money than men. Do you watch the news? In politics, men kiss women on the cheek and shake the hands of the other men. It's demeaning." Jess took a sip of his water. I kept my mouth shut. "I face sexism every single day in my office," he continued. "My entire life I've watched and experienced women taking the back seat to men. This has defined me. What would it say to young girls growing up now if I walked away and said I'm not here to help?"

I was speechless, awed by his gift for persuasive articulation and admiring of the role model he aspired to be. I finally understood that for Jess one of the greatest battles of his life was for the progress of women, and being recognized as one, even if he didn't feel like one, kept him active in the fight. I might've asked if he could make his political statement in other ways, like boycotting Hooters, rather than using his very body, except there was no point in continuing our friendly sparring. That was my own internal question. I was shadowboxing with myself.

The cat hopped up onto the footrest in the living room, crumpling the newspaper. "Oh yeah, Roscoe," Jess turned on his cat voice. "You gonna read the paper? Is that what you're going to do tonight?"

"He's gonna hang out with me," I said. "Someone's gotta do it."

"Oh yeah, Roscoe, you gonna hang out with auntie-uncle tonight?"

Jess looked directly at me and dropped his voice a few octaves to human range. "Hey, do you want to just be uncle?"

I nodded. "Yeah. I do."

Roscoe unfurled himself, more lion than cat, and licked one of his paws. Just thinking of myself as uncle made me like Roscoe a tiny bit more. Maybe I'd even let him into my room sometime.

"I'm sorry," Jess said. "I should've asked sooner."

"It's okay," I said. It was only then, when the focus of gendered language fell upon me, that I realized my hold on biology-pronoun agreement was more than a reliance on unbreakable rules. There was so much at stake. For Jess, it was the inescapable patriarchal history of our culture, the sexism still alive and rampant, and for me it was my social ties to women, developed through a lifetime of sports. I may not have missed my A-gays, nor my days on the soccer field with them, but dropping the "auntie" part distanced me even more from them, pushed me further into the unknown. To let go and take that step, I had to bring my longstanding connection to women with me, as well as Jess's speech on equality, keeping a firm grip on my own incipient sense of responsibility. And so I did become an "uncle" to Roscoe, unable to resist the term that sounded most perfect for me. "You know, it hadn't occurred to me the 'uncle' thing would feel so right until you said it."

Jess smiled that cockeyed grin of his. "Did we just have a gender moment?"

Thinking about our queering of the Hallmark moment, my own smile spread. I'd been treating gender as a foundation, moments piled on top of each other to create a base, a solid, unshakeable truth about who I was, when I could've just as easily considered these moments independently, as fleeting connections. For Jess and me, gender wasn't static. I could be "she" at work and "uncle" to the cat and Jess could be a politically identified woman whom I referred to as "he." "Yeah, I think we just did," I said.

Later that night, I added a high school photo of my own to the refrigerator, next to Monster's senior picture and Bec's prom picture, and the newest one of Jess wearing a white off-the-shoulder dress and holding a bouquet of roses. In my picture, I'm wearing a floral skirt and a baggy peach-colored silk shirt that resembles a T-shirt, as all my dress-up clothes did, my long brown hair flowing over my shoulders. With my facial expression, I'm cheerfully flipping the camera the bird, as if to say, "Come on, what are you looking at?" I may not have been unhappy, or maybe I was just happy enough, but the way I felt back then didn't matter; my history didn't define me forever, nor was it laid to rest in some girly graveyard. As I stuck the magnet to my photo, I recognized the young woman in the picture, felt her life inside of me, and knew it would remain there, wherever I went.

Seven

THE QUEER BIRDS
AND THE BEES

I passed my final semester of grad school reading and writing, writing and reading, reading and writing, taking breaks only to attend class and report to my job. Whole weeks would go by where I'd barely see my housemates. Winter disappeared and spring showed up, but I was too busy to notice. I did notice that after almost a year and a half, my "temporary" copywriting contract at the bank, long past its expiration, was going to continue indefinitely unless I terminated it. Burnt out from full-time school and mind-numbing, soul-deadening work that consisted of composing variations of, "Please select your account from the drop-down menu," in March I informed my company that I'd be leaving in early May. I planned to live off my recently acquired savings while finishing my thesis over the summer, and although I was nervous about walking away from a well-paid cubicle job, I also believed I was focusing on my passion.

I felt driven by my desire to write, to explain and make sense of my gendered experience, and I sought out connections with other people seeking to understand themselves and the world through words, mostly my writing peers at school. Over the course of the semester, I'd built a classroom-based friendship with Ramona, the sharp girl from my literature class who intrigued me even more in our workshop with her nonfiction stories about breaking into factory farms, staging demonstrations, and bailing other animal rights activists out of jail. I took notice that she referred to the guy she'd been dating when we first met as her "boyfriend at the time,"

97

and that her feedback on my essays about packing, testosterone, and binding was spot-on.

By sharing my personal explorations with Ramona and the others, my classmates had become confidants and friends. Nobody besides them, not my A-gays nor The Boys, knew about "Nick," the name that had popped into my head as sort of a boy alter ego. His arrival was so uneventful, I couldn't remember if I was sitting on the toilet or scrubbing my pits in the shower when he showed up. He played no role in my daily life, unlike my other alter ego, "Fun Nina," whom I'd created to channel the mood of my impending unemployed freedom, and to entertain Ramona by making fun of my former elderly bedtime, "Just Say No" policy to social events, and general fuddy-duddiness.

Ramona reminded me of a big kid with her department store backpack, Chuck Taylor sneakers, and round and youthful, near-angelic face—one you don't picture screaming "Your Mother Kills Puppies" into a bullhorn. But there was definitely something bad-ass about her, hinted at by the dark eye makeup she slathered on to appear at least her age. My youngest friend by far, she turned twenty-three at the end of the semester and threw a birthday party that served as the coming-out event for "Fun Nina."

Ramona lived with a crew from college in a futuristic three-story house, the living room like a spaceship with its trapezoidal window cove, modern fireplace, and tubular chimney. None of them could afford the place, so one person lived illegally in the unfinished garage and another had moved into the loft, using a thin shower curtain as a door. Ramona scored the best room, the only one on the main floor, because she was the mature leader of the group, the same role she held in her family as the oldest of three kids.

She told me this at her party, where we sat next to each other on her bed, sipping jungle juice, surrounded by our mutual writer friends. Her fine shoulder-length hair had been tinted auburn for the occasion, a perk of assistant managing a salon, and a long red scratch ran down her upper arm. She'd injured herself getting ready, squeezing into a revealing yellow dress from a store I associated with tweens. I couldn't make any sense of her fashion or style, what she was going for or whether she succeeded. But when she opened her mouth, damn was she cool.

Whatever the subject—movies, music, current events, books—she had something insightful and progressive to offer. She was the type who sent friends songs from undiscovered bands, the best clips from *The Daily Show* and *The Colbert Report,* and the top YouTube videos of the week, who stayed up to all hours surfing the Interwebz, as she called it, tinkering around late at night, getting cool while I slept.

She was also independent, leaving her date—a nerdy but nice enough guy she'd met online—in the living room to fend for himself. "We're not really dating," she said, scooting a bit closer to me. "I'm just using him for sex."

I could tell right away that guy wanted to date her, but she wasn't going to leave my left side all night if I kept up the entertainment. I told her about the two girls playing musical chairs for the seat on my right side. Both of them had once declared crushes on me and then gone into homo-panic mode when I responded with interest. Ramona had little patience or respect for their trepidation, which made me wonder if she was trying to tell me something about her sexuality. It didn't matter. Girls were always trying to tell me something about their sexuality, only to lose their nerve later.

"Watch her pinky," Ramona said under her breath. "It's crawling over to you. Look, she won't cross that third square. See, see, it's vibrating."

Low and behold, this girl's pinky was doing the same two-steps-forward, one-step-back dance near my thigh she'd done with me for the past year.

"It's not worth it," Ramona said. "If her pinky's prude, you're screwed. And I don't mean that literally."

"I think you may be funnier than me," I said.

"What do you mean 'may be'?"

After the party, we continued our comedy competition through daily e-mails that, although undoubtedly flirtatious, were more of a test of each other's wit, timing, and creative writing abilities. As part of our exchange, she sent me her online dating profile. Instead of the typical seductive or girl-next-door photo, she'd posted an adorable picture of herself with her hands clawed over an enormous vegan ice cream sundae, ready to pounce.

Mentally checked out of work, I used my last days in my cubicle to complete the quizzes on the dating site. Gender choices were limited to female and male, which I now considered sex assignments at birth, not genders, and the available orientations were straight, gay, and bisexual. Utilizing my SAT prep course training, I chose the "best option available": "bisexual male." I explained this to Ramona when I sent her my quiz results along with my critique of the options, the only paragraph in our two-week online exchange in which I felt forced to take a humorless, heavy tone. I was frustrated that a serious explanation was required, and that to anyone other than Ramona, who'd read sixty pages about me in our writing workshop, my choice would've made no sense.

To belatedly celebrate Cinco de Mayo, as well as the end of the school semester, one of our classmates threw a Seis de Mayo party. It was one of those rare summery days, blistering hot, even out by the beach, and I camped out on the back deck with a margarita in hand. While chatting away with my fellow writers about all the work we should've been doing, I kept catching myself checking the sliding-glass door for Ramona's arrival. Each time I looked, I reprimanded myself with a lecture that concluded with: Do NOT pursue another straight girl. Even if Ramona was different from the other I-want-to-but-I-can'ts, the last thing my nascent gender identity needed was to be the object of some twenty-three-year-old's lesbian awakening.

The moment Ramona arrived, I jumped up to greet her, forgetting all about my mandate. I followed her to the kitchen where she handed me one of the zucchini and mango tamales she'd prepared. The food display, which included a whale carved out of a watermelon and filled with fruit, was almost as majestic as the centerpiece in the living room. From a polished silver tray, a bottle of blue agave tequila rose, towering above a dozen shot glasses. We were standing too close when our host opened the bottle. "I don't do shots," I said, taking a step back.

"'Fun Nina' doesn't do shots?" Ramona taunted.

I held up my margarita cup to show the inch of liquid still left on the bottom. She held up hers to show the same before tilting it back and downing the rest. The ice cubes clanked against her teeth. "Your turn," she said.

"Are you trying to get me drunk?" I asked.

"Yes," she replied without hesitation. Then she laughed self-consciously. "It's not like you have to work tomorrow."

"Or this week. Or next week." I sucked down the rest of my drink and joined her for a shot. Which turned into another. And maybe another. We must've stopped once the bottle was empty. By then, the sun had fallen. Ramona's roommate, Katrina, a party tagalong who'd recently broken up with her boyfriend and required a lot of attention, ushered us from the deck to the living room. A fire was crackling in the fireplace.

"Let's play a game," she said, pulling Ramona and me down to the hearth. A petite brunette, Katrina had mischievous, trouble-seeking eyes. I liked her because she reminded me of myself at her age—functional yet out of control with a creative spirit she'd probably harness once she stopped mainlining cheap wine.

Still holding our hands, she leaned forward. With the flames blazing behind her, she looked possessed, like a horny imp. "Who's the cutest boy here?" she asked.

I paused to give the question serious consideration. "It's really not the best dude showing," I finally said.

"You're just bummed Joshua's not here," Ramona teased. I'd made no secret about my narcissistic crush on the stocky, neurotic Jewboy who could've been my twin brother.

A piece of wood snapped in the fireplace. We all flinched. They each gripped my hand tighter. Ramona didn't let go. "Well, I think

Nina is the cutest boy here," she said. Her green eyes turned crys-
talline in the firelight. I turned to Katrina. Her jaw rested open. I
looked down and stroked the frayed end of my cargo cutoffs. The
hair on my legs had grown in brown and thick, like that of a boy,
like the cutest boy there. Even through my blitzed haze, I felt the
colossal power behind Ramona's words, her validation all the more
pronounced because no girl had ever acknowledged me in that way
before. She might as well have said, "Open sesame."

I remember the two of us kissing on the railing of the deck
outside and on the long train ride back to her house, and in her
bed, where I woke up the next morning. Okay, I do remember
more than that, but drunk sex is kind of like drunk driving: you
bury it afterward, thankful nobody got hurt, knowing you did
things you wouldn't ordinarily do, and hope it's never mentioned
again. With the sun pounding through the bedroom window and
into my skull, I asked Ramona if it would be all right if I left.

"Go," she said. "I think I'm still drunk."

I got up and dressed quickly, stuffing my binder into the back
pocket of my pants. I pecked her on the lips good-bye.

"Hey," she called out when my hand was on the doorknob.
"Congrats on getting laid."

"I couldn't have done it without you," I replied reflexively.
The banter, the intoxicated oopsy-daisy sex, the fleeing, that was
all second nature to me. I closed her bedroom door behind me
and looked down the long hallway into the living room spaceship.
What now? I thought. I tipped my head back against her door.
What now?

Later that night, I rationalized myself out of attempting to date
Ramona with a laundry list of concerns: she was young, with no
real life experience; she wasn't athletic; she didn't ride a bicycle;
we had little in common besides writing; she lived like she was
in college; she was really, really young. Maybe I flowed down my
river of reasons to spare myself the pain of starting a relationship

that would, in my mind, undoubtedly end, or maybe I was trying to spare myself the anxiety that came with physical intimacy, but I always had my reasons, and all they'd ever left me with was a headache.

This time, I did my best to let my brain rest and did what all the kids were doing. I purchased my first text-messaging plan and put my thumbs in charge. When Ramona sent me a text every few hours, I'd simply respond with something witty. By evening, I'd be at a bar with her and Katrina, on her post breakup bender, and by late night, I'd be in Ramona's bed. It took two weeks for us to finish an evening closer to my house and end up in my bed.

It was the middle of the night and the glow from the streetlamp seeped through the thin blinds, lending us a dim light. Ramona tucked the corner of the pillow underneath her head, pressing her cheek into the feathers. The yellow cotton of my auto mechanic T-shirt crawled up around her neck. I fought the urge to take in Ramona, in my clothes and in my bed, as if once I did, she'd vanish, drop me for someone that made sense, like an actual dyke, or something uncomplicated, like a walking erection. "Why do you even like me?" I asked, immediately embarrassed by my vulnerability. "Wait, don't answer that."

She inched her pillow closer to mine and surprised me by playing along, assuaging my insecurity with a short list of my better traits. "But mostly I like you because we're from the same tribe," she said. "You feel familiar, like we've known each other for a long time."

I touched her cheek. Her skin was so smooth, untainted by life, yet there was something old and wise inside. I thought about smell chemistry, previous lives, cosmic ties, all the mysterious reasons people connect, everything that defied the explanations I craved. Despite myself, I liked her.

It was only later, when our mutual writer friends or the few A-gays I still spoke to outside of the larger group asked if Ramona was even a dyke, that I considered her tribe statement profound. I would always reply, "No, she's vegan." Sure, I was being a smart ass, but in a way Ramona's eating habits did seem relevant, as did her upbringing in a born-again Christian cult until she was a teenager. It was part of my tribe theory that she was so used to living on the outside, as other, that her feelings for me didn't trip up her place in the larger world she'd never really been part of anyway. And besides, it was a crucial part of our relationship that Ramona saw me as a cute boy, not a dyke, from the get-go.

During those first few weeks of sex, Ramona ignored my breasts as if they'd been redacted, and yet they still harassed me. If I wasn't wearing a binder or a sports bra, every time they moved, I could feel a sense of my own presence slipping away, an awareness of being inside my body fading, my old hookup autopilot trying to take over. But now that I'd met others like myself, I respected my own physical discomfort, treated it as real and valid, and sleeping with someone who accepted this as a premise for being with me empowered me to make adjustments. When disturbed by my breast-hang, I'd mutter my annoyance and pull her on top of me, or sometimes I'd just keep my binder or sports bra on in bed.

As I offered more verbal and physical cues, Ramona began to pick up on, and test ways to touch my chest with an "Is this okay?" I liked it when she ran her palm down the hard center line of my sternum or stroked a flat outstretched hand across my binder. When I shared that I had crazy awesome nipple sensation, but complained that any action there triggered an uncomfortable awareness of my breasts, Ramona reminded me that everyone has nipples. This helped me to close my eyes and hold on to my self-image, visualize my hard, flat chest while she touched me there. We could've compiled a rulebook for acceptable positions, but in the end there was only one: enforce my understanding of myself, my internal reality, that I had a dude-like chest.

A super-sexual person, Ramona had humped her bed while reading the Bible as a child, and as I teased her, had probably rode her umbilical cord in the womb. With our increasingly constant sex, I was struggling to maintain the necessary mind-set to stay present with the booby traps around every bend in my body. To avoid giving her a complex, I kept the depth of my challenges to myself until one night, when my roommates congratulated me on my one-month anniversary with Ramona. Erin had moved out immediately after her breakup with Bec six months before, and now it was only Jess, Melissa, and me, paying a bit more rent for some extra peace. Jess and Melissa were in the living room, telling me how proud they were of my one-month sex streak, and it set me off.

"I can't take it anymore," I exploded on to the two of them. "I feel like I'm having lesbian sex."

"What the heck does that mean?" Melissa asked.

Remaining in the kitchen, I took a few steps closer to the couch where they sat with their laptops, and let my mounted frustrations spill out. "There's just so many tits in the bedroom. Four of them. And mine are soooo much bigger," I whined. "They take up all the space in the room."

Melissa laughed in her half-amused, half-bemused way. Her breasts were huge, and I waited for her to concur, but only Jess nodded, prodding me to continue.

"It's like even when I'm in the moment, I'm watching from the outside," I said. "And all I can see are two people with the same bodies. Women."

Now they were both nodding. Only Melissa spoke. "Isn't there any way you could, I don't know, get out of your head and stop watching?"

"I'm trying," I complained. "But when I stop thinking, I tend to feel things more." I told them about a fucked up word I'd learned in Costa Rica for lesbian. "*Tortillera.* It means tortilla or something," I said, mashing my palms together. "And every time my crotch rubs up against her body, it's like I hear . . ." I began to smack my hands together. "You. Don't. Have. A. Dick." With my outburst came such a release of energy, of shame, that I felt calmer.

"Have you tried packing?" Jess asked.

Despite my initial excitement over my soft-pack experiment during the fall, I eventually found it annoying to have an artificial object in my briefs—don't even get me started on riding my bike with it. But still, it had transformed my perception of that area of my body. What had once been my orgasm button, useful only to that end, was now something I could relate to if I thought of it as a teeny weeny, a mini-dick. Ramona was well aware of this, but neither of us reinforced it, and I had trouble holding on to my crucial self-understanding when I caught my dick looking like a pussy and rolling around made me feel like a tortilla. Even language failed to anatomically separate us since Ramona used the word *beej* on the receiving as well as the giving end; as she'd astutely pointed out, there's no direct object equivalent to a blow job for women.

"I tried my softie once, at the very beginning," I told Jess. Instead of my typical evasive crotch squirreling, I'd been able to comfortably press my bulge into her. "It was great until she grabbed me there and I panicked. I was all, 'It doesn't do anything.' I think I scared her."

"You need a strap-on," Jess said.

I sighed deeply and leaned back against the stove. The gas knob nailed me in the tailbone. Awesome, I thought, I'm going to need a goddamn costume change to have sex. What would I say? Excuse me for a sec while I suit up and swap my dick out—my boner is in the other room?

"Don't look so dejected," Melissa said. "This isn't a bad thing. It's a good thing."

I was pretty sure everyone—Jess, Melissa, and plenty of lesbians—had strap-on sex. Ramona had even had strap-on sex, with cisgender guys, bend-over boyfriends. I considered myself decent with my hands and mouth, but that was like being a hurdler and pole vaulter, good at two events when I wanted to be good at all of them, a decathlete. I was embarrassed to be so inexperienced, too old to be learning new tricks, nearly a thirty-year-old virgin.

I stormed off to my bedroom and returned to the living room, dropping my milk crate of useless toys on to the carpet with a thud. I pulled out each dildo—a marbled pink one, a double-sided blue swirly one, another long and ribbed one—for my roommates to reject with no argument from me. Had I been into sex toys, perhaps I would've used one years ago, but wearing a polka-dotted corkscrew would only ever have exacerbated the dickless awareness I tried to avoid. My stash, which was too dormant to bother me before, now taunted me with its ridiculousness. I held up a red and silver glittery harness. "I can't wear this, right?"

"Not unless you have a cape to go with it," Jess said.

There was no way I could do it in sparkles. I packed the stiff plastic harness back into the crate and carelessly tossed the dildos on top.

"The key is to find something that suits you, that you can connect with, so it's yours. You," Jess said.

Having gone down the soft-pack road, I understood the importance of connection, and once again, Jess agreed to escort me to Good Vibes.

In my room, I stacked my milk crates in opposite order—snowboarding gear on the bottom, biking gear in the middle, and sex gear on top. Across the pile I draped a patterned textile from my travels in Asia, nostalgic for the time when my only concerns for the day were what I would eat and where I would sleep, basic human needs that distracted me from another one—comfort in my body.

On Saturday morning, about to enter Good Vibes with Jess, I received my hourly hello text from Ramona. I texted back my hello and my location, along with, "Any requests?" and headed directly to the far wall with its display of realistic cocks. I passed over the Lone Star, Mustang, and Outlaw, renaming them stubby, boomerang, and hung like a horse, and picked up the relatively large Bandit. I ran my hand over the cut head, the textured arch of the shaft, the balls that made the base. At a hundred dollars, it was expensive, but what other choice did I have—unlike most of my clothing, I couldn't buy one of these used.

My phone vibrated. "No veins, balls, or flesh colors," the text read.

I replied right away, banging out the letters: "There's no way I'm getting some iridescent purple dolphin or twitching rabbit foo foo." I shoved my phone into my pocket, pushing down my fear that Ramona and I were approaching an impasse, the veiny deal breaker.

I moved along the wall and my eyes landed on a black harness with silver buckles. I unclipped the apparatus from the hanger and slipped it on over my jeans. I tightened the waist straps and galloped over to Jess, turning a few times as if on a catwalk.

"I find it remarkable that for as little sex as you have, you're totally comfortable parading around with a harness," Jess said.

I was the opposite of comfortable. "Is it even on right?"

Jess nodded yes and explained the features to me. Then, for a few minutes, I obsessed over the pros and cons of this harness before Jess reminded me that it wouldn't be the only one I ever owned, just my first.

My phone buzzed. Ramona's text read: "Of course you want a dick that looks real. And I want my fantasy dick. Get what you need and we'll figure it out. Just make sure it's big enough :)."

With that kind of encouragement, I grabbed a plastic tube with the Bandit, not caring that it only came in the root-beer color. I also purchased the black leather harness, even though it felt like a jerk move to bring a dead cow to bed with a vegan, especially one willing to meet my needs.

I laid the harness on my bed and, afraid that if I took it apart I'd never be able to put it together again, I decided to just loosen the four buckles. I stepped into it like I had in the store, except this time I was pantless and my new cock jutted through the O-ring.

I tightened the buckles and bent over to touch my toes. I readjusted the buckles and did a lunge. I engaged in more harness calisthenics and made a variety of adjustments before giving up on a perfect fit and tucking the four excess strap ends into the waist. I wished sex seemed appealing; I felt like I was going spelunking with a lead pipe attached to my crotch. Then I tried on a pair of boxers, and without the buckles, doohickeys, and straps visible—with only the Bandit, bowed toward my right thigh and raising the plaid cotton—I saw it. Manifest hard-on. Oh, I was in the mood.

The next day in Ramona's bedroom, even with my jeans on over my boxers, the outline of my erection remained obvious. I'd already showed Ramona my items, shared with her my best stopwatch times for getting the rig on, and released so much angst that she must've been relieved when I shut up and kissed her. I was relieved. My worry disappeared the moment our lips touched, and I felt my whole body, one intact entity, drawn to her.

Finally, something in the room took up more space than my breasts. There was just no escape from the boner pushing through my jeans, screaming, "Pay attention to me." Ramona's confidence appeared to skyrocket with a place to put her hands, and where I had once done everything and anything to avoid looking at myself, now I couldn't even blink. I watched as she rubbed the base of her palm along the rise in my denim. As she wrapped her hand around the curve and squeezed, my mind fused the big guy to my mini-man underneath, jolting my groin awake.

Ramona undid the button on my jeans and slid the zipper down. The sound of the teeth unhooking rang in my ears. She reached inside my boxers and tugged the cock up, toward my belly button.

"Shit, you really know what you're doing," I said.

Ramona laughed. "I may have done this a few times."

On her bed, I lifted myself onto my knees, letting my jeans fall to the crook. Her hand worked inside my boxers, moving up and down. Focused so intently on the action, it took me a few seconds to realize I couldn't feel more than a gentle knocking against my pelvis. Reaching inside my fly, she pulled out the cock. Holding it in one hand, she ran her tongue over the tip. She wrapped her lips around the end and slid down the shaft.

I kept my eyes on her, trying not to think about what was actually in her mouth and how it tasted—like silicone, plastic, fake, not human. I hoped she wasn't thinking either. When I got too caught up thinking about what she was thinking, too focused on the root-beer color that wasn't my own skin, the buzzing stirred inside me, the voice that said: get out, get out now. I pulled back from her and distracted myself by grabbing hold of the dick and stroking it, alternating grips like dudes did in porn.

"That's hot," Ramona said. She removed what was left of her clothing and I peeled off my T-shirt. I reached toward the nightstand. "Should I wear a condom?" I asked.

"Why would you do that?" she answered.

I wasn't sure. "Bacteria?" I tried. "Or, I don't know, fuzz from my boxers?"

For a moment, her face softened, then her bed-humper eyes took over. "Do not put on a condom!" she demanded.

"I like it when you tell me what to do," I said with a smirk. I removed only the lube from the drawer and rubbed some on the cock before going down on her, something that usually quieted my mind completely. But now nervous thoughts invaded: I had absolutely no rhythm, couldn't even clap along to songs, was the worst dancer. What if I was physically incapable of doing this? Ramona hit me on the shoulder. "Fuck me. Now."

I rose to her face and kissed her before she guided the cock inside of her. I couldn't feel much down there except the space between us fading away as she pulled me in deeper, opening her mouth in pleasure. Soon, I was sweating, concentrating so hard on thrusting that I couldn't possibly pay attention to anything else. The base of the cock, the balls, hit against my pubic bone, helping with control but little in the way of feeling.

When her bed started to squeak, we both giggled. I wrapped my hands around the top side of the mattress for leverage. I wished I was bigger and stronger than her, that I had ab muscles and stamina. I was too focused on getting the job done to enjoy myself, and felt only relief that she came before I had a coronary. Afterward, she didn't want me to move, so I collapsed, resting all of my weight on her. Both of us were coated in sweat, our bodies stuck together around my Frog Bra.

Once we caught our breath, she suggested we try a position where I could see the cock going in and out. She rose to her hands and knees and I set myself up behind her. From this angle, I could see everything. And my eyes nearly bugged out at what I saw.

A dick, my dick, was moving inside of her.

Ramona's three favorite activities were sleeping, eating, and fucking. This was something she'd say with proud hedonism and her self-conscious belly laugh, as if she knew there were more important things in life, she just didn't care. Forever a student, she treated the summer like she always had, as vacation. Even without classes, she maintained the same hours at the salon, and while she had independent study coursework, her only goal was to produce first draft material for her thesis, whereas I had to finish mine. For the few hours a day she was at work, I wrote at her house or her local coffee shop, which left us with an enormous amount of time to spend the rest of the summer perfecting her three favorite activities.

Once I embraced my dick, which I decided called for a dorky, Jewish name, like "Isaac," sex monopolized our time. Ramona could get me to do anything, as long as she enticed me with the comment, "Boys love this." I always enjoyed her suggestions, but I also appreciated that she included me in the collective of cis boys—a group she was physically attracted to—and wasn't just calling me a "boy" to placate me. We threw role playing into the mix, occasionally cowriting detailed scripts with me assuming well-developed characters like a faggy frat boy and a middle school student who gets a special lesson from his math teacher. This was lighthearted fun, but for me it was also more, a safe space to explore boy phases, an opportunity to express the types of guys that lived inside of me.

When we weren't fucking, we were eating. We shopped at the farmer's market, and together we'd make stir-fries with tempeh, nut sauces, fruit salads, and baked goods from *Vegan Cupcakes Take Over the World*. We also created a vegan-friendly restaurant circuit. The best was Sunday mornings when Ramona would roll over all sleepy eyed and request brunch at the Pork House for their killer tofu scramble.

To recover from all the eating and sex, we slept a lot, or at least rested, almost always at Ramona's house because her room had more privacy than mine. We often opened the huge window beside her bed, watched the breeze rustle the leaves on the bougainvillea tree, and pretended we were outside. Sometimes we wrote like this as well, sitting next to each other in our matching writing uniforms—navy-blue hooded sweatshirts—typing away on our laptops with the occasional chuckle to ourselves.

Art parties at her salon, literary events, lazing around the park, vegging out in front of the TV—the activity didn't matter, the adventure was Ramona. We had constant repartee, gave everything a sexual innuendo, and could discuss books, writing, and the merits of the Michaels—Ondaatje, Chabon, Cunningham, and Lewis—for hours on end.

At the end of the summer, I turned in my thesis, officially finishing graduate school. I rewarded myself by planning a trip to visit my best friend from college in Scotland, with a preliminary stop on the East Coast to visit my parents and my brother. Like gay pride weekend, a week with my parents always seemed like a good idea until it dragged on and on, ended in exhaustion, and left me swearing I'd never participate again, only to forget by the following year. Had I not been leaving Ramona for three weeks, I probably would've been more excited about the entire trip. But when you're in that relationship phase where you sing along to Top 40 love songs on the radio, leaving your girlfriend isn't the best idea.

Neither was bringing up the possibility of making out with other people while I was gone, which I did, about a week before I left in September. We were on her bed, pretending to be outdoors. She bit her lower lip and stared out the window. "I don't want to make out with other people," she said.

"It's just an option," I said, even though I had no interest in making out with anyone else either. I rarely, if ever, spoke honestly, or created any space between us, ignoring all my instincts to take time for myself, afraid both of being alone and of hurting her. But something about our approaching separation pushed me forward. As I watched her eyes fill with tears, my mouth moved without instruction. "I think of this as our first adult relationship," I said. "The first of many."

"Why do you have to be so negative, pessimistic?" she replied. "It's like you're always waiting for the other shoe to drop. Why can't you just enjoy this?"

"I am enjoying this," I said. Ramona fixed my collar, told me I was dreamy, cut my hair, and picked out my cologne; I was enjoying my third adolescence, after the high school one, after the dyke one. I was twenty-nine going on eighteen, with all the hope and happiness of a teenager falling in love for the first time, and all the maturity of someone who knows that first loves don't last forever. Or at least that this one wouldn't. "I'm sorry I brought it up," I said. "I'm so sorry."

Eight

HOMESICK

During the last few years, my former bedroom at my parents' house in New Jersey had turned into a repository for my father's junk—two televisions from the '80s, den furniture from a "country house" we once had in a townhouse community for NYC Jews, stacks of *Consumer Reports* and Elmore Leonard and Tony Hillerman paperbacks that busted out from every cabinet and shelf. The closet contained some of my father's clothes, the button-down shirts, khaki slacks, and corduroy pants I used to borrow. My dad sometimes slept there, the only downstairs bedroom, to avoid waking my mother up on early gym mornings, and the private bathroom held his razors, shaving cream, and Irish Spring soap.

I couldn't complain about the loss of my room since I only slept there during one of our semiannual get-togethers, the other usually at a vacation destination. I wasn't sure which was creepier, that I crashed in my dad's storage room/bachelor pad suite or that he slept surrounded by my high school artifacts, a version of me frozen in time as a teenager. One entire wall, a painted bulletin board, still held hundreds of pushpins with my varsity letters, team pictures, athletic plaques, newspaper articles, and photos of me and my high school friends. This wall was the only evidence I'd lived in that room for the three years after our family moved from New York.

On the first morning of my East Coast trip, after exchanging little more than a hello with my parents, they lent me their Lexus to visit my brother in New Hampshire. They were always thrilled to aid our sibling time, contributing money, cars, plane tickets, anything, and had intended for our close relationship before I'd been conceived, planning us a little over three years apart, hoping for a girl and a boy. When I was ten years old, my parents told me a story about one morning at our country house a few years earlier. They'd left my brother and me asleep in the room we shared while they played their regular tennis doubles game and returned home to find that I'd dressed him in mismatched clothes and had put him in his booster seat, where I was feeding him mashed bananas.

I couldn't remember this early caretaking incident, but when I heard about it, I held on to it, built it into the foundation of great pride I took in being a big sister. I continued to watch over my brother at sleepaway camp, Club Med kids club, and ski school, and when he was still in high school I started taking him backpacking abroad with me. Even if he couldn't find our destination on a map, as long as I promised to send detailed packing instructions, he'd go anywhere with me—my mom gave him the nickname, "Monkey see, Monkey do." He turned out to be my best travel partner and the best gift my parents had ever given me. His friends called him "Kriegs," I always called him my brother, bro, or dude, and in the rare instances I had to use his name, Eric, it sounded weird to me.

He and his girlfriend, Sarah, had just moved from Jackson Hole to a microscopic New Hampshire town for their first "real jobs," as my mom put it. My brother worked in admissions and Sarah taught history at the local boarding school. Their new home, school property on the outskirts of campus, was pure New England farmhouse with white clapboard, shuttered windows, and a barn attached to their living quarters. The inside of their place was like a glorified dorm room, decorated with the same Bob Dylan and ski-racing posters, tapestries and Buddhist mandalas, collegiate sports photos and plaques that had graced the walls of our shared home three winters before—a living experience I treasured as the first time my brother and I were equals, our age-difference inconsequential, true friends.

When I arrived, they were preparing to head out to the school's "family dinner"—a biweekly formal affair. My brother, situationally forced to be in a clean-cut phase, had his Jewfro trimmed to stockbroker length and his long, thin face freshly shaven. With his broad shoulders and lean body, he looked handsome in his tie and blazer, yet too cookie cutter for my taste, blanched of personality, like he'd donned the uniform of well-bred man. For as much as I looked forward to spending time with him, I tended to forget about that initial moment of disappointment when I realized he was still enmeshed in the stodgy environment and culture that I'd escaped. "You look like Dad," I said.

"It's 'cause these are his clothes." He pulled up the loose slacks and buckled his belt a notch tighter. "Twice a week we have to do this shit."

Sarah was one of those naturally beautiful women, no makeup required, and a world-class athlete. About five years ago, when she'd first started dating my brother, he told me, "She's just like you but less pissy," which I discovered to be true, at least in the sporty ways. Instead of her usual jock wear, she had on a plain brown V-neck sweater and a modest patterned skirt. "How do you do it?" I asked. "Don't the skirts kill you?"

"I don't mind wearing skirts," Sarah said. "But these dinners are a bit much. We're supposed to engage the kids in 'meaningful conversations' about world events."

"Fourteen-year-olds don't want to talk about the Iraq War." My brother loosened his tie slightly. "And after working all day, I don't want to force them to, either."

"At least we get to sit together," Sarah said. "They had to make an exception for us since we're not married."

This academy, catering to kids who'd had some disciplinary problems or struggled in other schools, was even stricter with its rules than I'd expected. My brother had already warned me about the evening's "skirts for girls" and "jacket and tie for boys" requirement, and I'd opted out, bringing my own food to prepare.

"You're lucky you don't have to go to this dinner," my brother said as I snapped a few photos of him with his arm wrapped around Sarah.

After they ambled down the porch and the screen door slammed behind them, I poured out my bag of vegetables. I did feel lucky to skip the stuffy, uptight event; I'd always felt relieved to avoid formal affairs. I recalled the picture on my wall that had caught my eye the previous night, taken before my senior prom. In it, my three best friends are in their evening gowns, gloves, and costume jewelry, and I am in a baggy striped shirt and jeans. Guys had asked me to go and my friends had begged me, but envisioning myself in a prom dress was too horrific and actually wearing one impossible to bear. I kept my dress terror a secret because I believed what my mom, a woman who seemed disinterested in femininity but who desired to fit in nonetheless, had told me growing up: "Honey, wearing dresses is what girls do. It's the respectable thing to do."

I found a knife in a drawer and chopped the zucchini, hitting the cutting board with rhythmic bangs. I sautéed the pile of pale green slivers with mushrooms and onion while my pasta boiled. Steam filled the kitchen and I opened the window to a damp fall breeze. Eating my dinner alone, I listened for the din of teenagers, their bursts of laughter, and felt my own loss and regret for all the fun I'd missed.

The next morning in the cafeteria, while scooping Cheerios from the bulk bin into my bowl, I felt a tap on my shoulder. I turned around to find the wild red hair and rebelling skin of an adolescent boy. "Tuck your shirt in," he commanded.

I quickly placed my bowl on the counter and pushed the bottom of my thrift store collared shirt into the top of my zip-off travel pants. I heard the laughter before I saw my brother at a nearby table, his open jaw vibrating in our familial guffaw. Sarah and the other faculty members at the table all stared at me with amused smiles on their faces.

I placed my tray down on their table and my brother explained the joke: only boys had to tuck in their shirts. The awkward aftermath of being seen as a guy, which often included an effusive apology, trumped any feelings I may have had about this frequent experience. Usually these interactions, mostly in restrooms, were with strangers. Nobody I cared about was ever around to find the situation hilarious. "Hardee-har-har," I mocked.

I chomped on my cereal in a silent, building rage. This place charged $30,000 a year, thirty-thousand dollars to provide kids with support, opportunity, and special help. Is this what adults believed created honorable kids—peer policing so that chromosomes matched polo shirts? And what was so wrong, or so funny, about someone like me, dressed in boys' clothes, being called out as a boy?

My anger festered while my brother was at work. It rained hard all day, and I stayed inside, revising an excerpt about testosterone from my thesis—the entirety of which I planned to give to my brother—to submit for a writing contest. I barely gave him a second to grab a beer out of the fridge when he returned home before I continued our conversation from that morning. "You know, people think I'm a boy all the time," I said.

"I don't see it." He kicked off his trail runners, threw his legs onto the New York Giants blanket that covered the futon, and turned on the TV.

"That I look like a boy. You don't think so?" Trying to get his attention, I leaned forward in my wicker chair—one of the many pieces of furniture he had inherited from our family's other country house, this one in the Hamptons. "Look at me," I said.

"What do you want me to say?"

I thought the answer was obvious. I flattened my chest, kept my hair short, wore no jewelry, dressed entirely in unisex clothes, and had a naturally masculine body comportment—what more could be done? "I want you to acknowledge that I do look like a boy."

"Well, to me, you don't." He found the channel with the Rangers pregame before flipping through more channels and settling on women's tennis for the interim before face-off.

"Dude!" I said. "I drove six hours to visit you. You were gone all day. Do you want me to be here or do you want to watch TV?"

"Sorry, I'm just trying to relax."

Whether it was our genetic makeup or our upbringing, we were both always trying to relax. Even as kids, when we were supposed to be doing something fun or interesting, there was a race, trophy, admission test, an expectation to work harder and achieve more. He probably had it bad at his first "real" job—the internal pressure found its way into everything.

I asked him nicely to turn off the TV, promising him he could turn it back on when the game started, and he complied. When I was kind to him, he listened to me. I liked to believe that over the years, I'd earned his trust. In his struggles with "bad" grades (aka Bs), puberty, dating, and college essays, he'd always called me for help. I'd give him a pep talk, purposefully ignoring anything he could've done better by pointing out only the good, right, hopeful, and positive in whatever was happening. To hear him say, "Thanks, I feel better now," made me feel better—we had the same self-judgment, fears, worries, and concerns. I saw so much of myself reflected in him. "What if I want to be a boy?" I said.

"I don't understand what you mean by that. I can't pretend to understand what it's like to be gay."

He splayed open his hand and focused on what was once a callus and was now his favorite spot to pick. Mine was my thumb. We had the same anxious tics, the same mannerisms and gestures, the same huge hands. Looking at his broad shoulders, powerful trap muscles, collarbone straight and hard, I could see myself inside his boy body. "It's about being a boy," I said. "This has nothing to do with being gay."

"To me, it's the same thing. Maybe this makes sense in San Francisco, but I don't live in your world. If you were sitting around with all my friends, watching a hockey game, you wouldn't look like a boy, or be a boy, or whatever."

I thought of his friends from Jackson Hole, pounding cases of watery beer, talking about girls and sex in that ignorant "where's the clit" way, insulting anyone wearing pink with a "fag" slur, pissing off the back porch out of laziness, and topping it off with a burping war. Many of them were nice guys, but I didn't want to be one of them. I just thought I looked like them. "If I wanted to blend in with your friends, I could take testosterone. I've been doing research. This is what I write about." My voice rose in frustration. "That's all it takes, one hormone to be seen as a guy."

He looked at his palm again, about to pick.

"Don't," I said.

He squeezed his hand into a fist. "You know you'd break Dad's heart."

"Are you fucking serious?" He'd broken our only rule, our one unspoken sibling code—protection from our parents. We gave to each other what our parents' dreams for us prevented them from giving us—unconditional support. We took care of each other, or at least I took care of him. "You know what happened when I started dating Jennifer in college."

"I'm sorry."

"Dad said it was like someone had taken a knife and cut his heart out," I said, repeating his very words as if I could make my brother feel my burden.

"I'm sorry. I know. Really, I shouldn't have used Dad's guilt shit on you." My brother nodded his head aggressively in self-beration. "Look, it's my issue," he said. "I wouldn't know how to explain to my friends that my sister is now my brother. I don't want to have to explain that. I know, it's selfish, I know it is."

My appreciation for his honesty was dulled by his self-absorption, his ignorance of what I'd have to go through should I ever truly consider such a change.

"But why do you have to write about this?" he asked. "Why can't you write about traveling?"

In his whine, I heard his embarrassment and desire for secrecy, an expression of my own self-consciousness and fear. "Anyone can write about traveling," I said.

"But why always the gay thing?"

"It's a gender thing!"

"Why this?"

The emotions surged, a tidal wave that hit so fast I didn't feel it coming until my hands were shaking and my face was quivering. "So some day a sister won't have to have this conversation with her brother," I screamed and ran out of the room.

In the bathroom, I turned on the water. I placed my hands on the counter and pressed forward toward the mirror. A boyish young woman stared back at me. I understood my brother's confusion. Even in my world, in San Francisco, a boyish young woman meant gay. We prided ourselves on our ability to read people in this manner, our gaydar triggered by any effeminate man or butch woman. I stared into the mirror at my face, my body, my reflection, searching for something to tell me I was fundamentally different from all the other dykes I resembled. When I found nothing, I turned off the water. Back in the living room, the Rangers game had started.

I returned to Jersey the following night, shortly after my father, a patent attorney, and my mother, an IT/network person who did things with computers she could never succinctly explain, arrived home from work. My mother was small and shrinking each year, or so she claimed, but what she lost in size she made up for with her huge presence. She was constantly whirling and had a mouth that fired like a machine gun. "Squash soup or bean salad for appetizer? How many shoots of asparagus? Quinoa hot or cold?" she shouted from the kitchen.

Before my dad or I could choose a question and shout back an answer, my mom pounded into the living room, a feat to make so much noise in only slippers. "How come nobody's answering me? What's the matter with you?" Her abrasive New York accent was even more grating when she was irritated. "Do you want eggplant or not?"

After thirty years of marriage, she didn't need to ask my dad about his food preferences. He'd eat anything as long as there was hot sauce and a snack of matzo while he waited. "Whatever's easiest for you," he replied. A laidback guy with a warm charismatic smile and olive skin that made him appear Sephardic, he'd retained the attractiveness of his youth despite the receding hairline, bushy eyebrows, and paunch that fluctuated depending on how much my mom nagged him about it.

"Honey?" my mom said to me.

"How about bean salad and eggplant," I said.

"That's it? What about quinoa? Asparagus? Do you want salad first?"

"Sure," I replied.

"You're going to eat *all* that food?"

"Mom, please. Any of it sounds good." It's not like she was cooking; she was only deciding which prepared gourmet food to microwave. "I'll eat whatever you put on my plate."

"That's just a lot of food," she repeated.

"If it's that much, then don't give it to me."

"You're no help." She pounded back into the kitchen.

Half an hour with my parents and I had a headache. The jabbering, the circular conversations, the shouting across rooms, the noise was constant. Even the background TV, the clicking between every cable news and finance channel, was chaos. Feeling the return of the aggro, pissy New Yorker in me I'd forgotten all about, I was even more annoyed. "Dad, pick one show, or turn off the TV."

"Geez, tough crowd," he said. That was one of his party jokes, an easy fallback around my mother and apparently me. My dad was an entertainer, social and affable, but also a closet introvert, a lone wolf who enjoyed going to the movies by himself and could go days with only books as company. We were similar in that way, and had so much in common, I shouldn't have been concerned about finding something to talk about when he turned off the TV, but we'd already discussed the rainy weather in more detail than meteorologists.

I considered the novel I was reading a possible topic, except the protagonist was a gay guy, and every movie or event I attended was with Ramona, whom I hated to bring up since my dad would only refer to my girlfriend as "my friend"—an insulting lack of acknowledgment, yet one I preferred to his previous woe-is-me melodrama—which made me partial to following our unofficial "Don't Ask, Don't Tell" policy of the last decade. I faced the conversation-starter dilemma every three weeks or so when I owed him a phone call. Sometimes I'd luck out and have a hemorrhoid or minor physical ailment to get us going, and for a while I'd been able to fill the rest of the space complaining about my job.

"Any chance your friend wants to hire you back at the bank?" my dad asked, breaking the silence. Compared to my mom, my dad could seem mute, but really he was just more efficient. He never wasted words. His questions were subtle, calculated, like chess moves.

"I quit for a reason," I said. "That job was killing my soul."

"I thought you left to finish your thesis."

I waited, hoping he might congratulate me on finishing, or ask what my thesis was about, or if he could read some of it, but he tended to ignore the parts of my life that mattered to me if they didn't matter to him. The only responses worse than his deliberate silences and guilt-trips were his psychotic rants in which he'd spew spittle and steam about how quitting piano or dropping pre-med amounted to "throwing my life away." He hadn't gone on a tirade in many years, so I wondered why I still looked at the spot I'd been sitting in when he smashed the footrest after I chose to play on an extra basketball team instead of my only softball team. But mostly, I wondered what it would take for me to forgive him and let go of my anger.

"I told you, Dad, every time we spoke for a year, how much I hated that job. You were there, right? Did you hear me?"

"It's a really good company," he said.

I'd explicitly and repeatedly told both my parents that leaving my job would allow me the space to forge a new path more in-line with my creative interests, investing in my writing would eventually open up new opportunities, and although the uncertainty scared me, I believed in myself and knew what was best for me. For the three months leading up to my final decision, they relentlessly picked away at it, made me second-guess myself with their ceaseless cynical interrogation: "Are you sure? What are you going to do? What if you can't get another job?" Even after I gave notice, my dad kept asking if I'd pursued all the options, like taking a short break or working from home.

Their inability to listen and support me while making a tough decision was so upsetting that I wrote them a letter, telling them how I wished they'd handled the situation. I wrote it entirely from their perspective, saying that as parents they only wanted what was best for me and were concerned that I was giving up a good job, but that they trusted me to make smart decisions for myself. My mom replied to my letter, "Honey! That's exactly what I meant to say!" My dad never replied; as my mom explained later, I had offended him. I understood then that my mom could be taught to give me what I needed and my dad could not. He required a heavy hand.

"I was miserable at that job," I said to him. "I saved money. It's over. And I don't want to talk about it ever again."

"Okay, okay. Forget I brought it up," he said, offended yet again.

"Dinner's ready!" my mom shouted.

The three of us sat at the same wooden table we'd had my entire life, a square, unbalanced without my brother, that formed the cornerstone of the Krieger Covenant. It had been our one household rule to eat dinner together because, according to my mom, that's what defined a family. This daily event also required my brother and me to answer any and all questions asked about us. In exchange for adhering to this simple procedure, my parents acted, and would continue to act, as a financial safety net forever should we need them. The auxiliary to the agreement, more habit than rule, was that we all shoveled our dinner into our mouths, as if racing to clear our plates, which tonight occurred in under three minutes.

"You haven't changed at all," my mom said. "You still eat too much. Are you going to work that off at the gym with me?"

My mom was the only person who thought calling me fat was an enticement to hang out with her. Which made me the only person who found that endearing. "If you're lucky," I said.

"Well, you just think about what you want to do for bonding time."

This "bonding time" was a staple of spending time with my mom. It entailed an activity alone together and culminated in a Q&A session for which she'd pick a topic related to my abnormalcy, like being gay or not wanting to birth children. She'd ask uncomfortable questions and try not to cry at the answers while I'd do my best to be thankful that we were having a difficult conversation instead of a fight, which between us was as common as breathing.

For the next two days while my parents were at work, I revised my contest submission and enjoyed the solitude in their absence. In the evenings, my dad watched the nightly news, and I sat with him because I knew how much joy it brought him to simply be in the same room with me. We shot the shit or kept quiet, which allowed him to project the version of me he kept in his head without the rude interruption of my actual self, and allowed me to hold on to our tranquil stalemate as the best connection I could have with my dad. Then we'd all go out to dinner, where my mom was liable to embarrass me with her rude tone toward the staff, as if the hostess meant to make us wait or purposefully seated us in a "bad" location, and I'd try to be mad at her but would only feel sad that she felt so constantly wronged.

On Friday, my last day before flying out to Scotland, my mom took the day off work. I decided on a shopping trip to the mall for bonding time, but regretted this choice when the fighting started less than two miles from the house. She had an upcoming wedding to attend and wanted to know if I'd help, or at least sit with her, while she searched for a dress.

Even before I opened my mouth, I knew I was being an asshole. "Would you ask Eric to go with you for a dress?"

"I don't know. Probably not," she said, as we passed the arched gates and ivy-laced stone buildings of the local university. "I just thought it'd be a nice thing for you to do with your mother."

We drove alongside the bright green fairways of a golf club that was supposedly classier than the club where my parents belonged. I wished I'd chosen to play nine holes with her or hit a few buckets at the driving range. We both preferred any sport over shopping. "Don't ask me to do something you wouldn't ask Eric to do," I said.

"Because it would be so much for you to do one thing for me." She kept her eyes on the road, her lower jaw jutted out, her whole mouth tense.

I gritted my teeth, struggling to keep calm. "Not. This. Thing."

"Not this, not that. Any excuse to be selfish. You don't want to do me a favor, fine. But don't make excuses, like you're offended to sit in a store and watch me try on dresses."

"Just because I'm your daughter doesn't mean I should be expected to go dress shopping with you. Would you ask Eric to go with you?" I repeated.

She turned into the mall parking lot and halted at the first stop sign. "I don't know. But if I asked, he would."

My mom was right. And if I were my brother, I would too. But I wasn't him. I was her daughter. "I hate dresses!" I said.

"You didn't hate your bat mitzvah dress," she countered. "You scooped that right up."

"That's 'cause it looked like a T-shirt!" I yelled. "And it had a mock turtleneck!"

I was completely astonished. How far removed could she have possibly been from my childhood to think that I liked that dress?

Or rather, how much had I kept to myself, trying to please her
and do the respectable thing. I started to spew incoherently about
female expectations and assumptions and my mom battled back
until we were so far from our starting point that silence was the
only recourse.

She turned off the ignition. "So, are we going in?"

I nodded.

I'm not sure if we apologized; sometimes we did, sometimes
we didn't.

The mall was a bust. I'd forgotten that in chain stores, men's smalls
were too large and women's clothes always had one fatal flaw, be
it a swooping neckline, pastel color, extra-short sleeves, or feminine contour. My mom bought me white athletic socks, running
shoes, and boxers, all of which even she found boring. "That's all
you want," she said. "You're no fun." Then I remembered that Jess
had recommended the untapered button-down shirts, a standard
men's style, sold at Brooks Brothers in women's sizes.

We found the store at another nearby mall. The saleswoman
greeted us with pursed lips. With a sweater tied around her neck,
just below her pearls, she was ready for croquet and caviar. Her
eyes probed me from my dirty sneakers to my ragged T-shirt to my
unkempt hair. Had I been alone, I would've left, but with my mom
and her credibility trailing, I walked to the back of the store and
found the untapered shirts. I tried on a few in the dressing room
and came out to show my mom a yellow checkered one that I liked.
She nodded her approval. "What are you wearing underneath?"
she asked. "Is that a sports bra?"

I'd been wearing the more comfortable Frog Bras around the
house, but shopping required a binder. Seeing even a slight round
of my chest underneath a shirt would deter me from buying it.
"Something like that." I walked into the dressing room and closed
the door.

I hit the children's section on the boys' side next, where I

NINA HERE NOR THERE   129

flipped through a stack of plain white button-downs, mumbling to myself about what size to try. With each shirt neatly pinned and folded with tissue paper, I wanted to avoid making a mess for the saleswoman who already disliked me. My mom called her over and asked what boys' size would be the same as a women's 6.

"There is no same," the saleswoman said. You could kill a rock with her glare.

Duh, I thought—boys' shirts are longer and narrower, the shoulders broader, the sleeves shorter—just give me a starting point.

"Fine," my mom said to her, using the harsh tone she reserved for people in the service industry, but this time it didn't mortify me. "If there is no same, what's the closest?"

The saleswoman looked like she might toss off her sweater shawl and throw down. I had no doubt my mom would kick her ass. The saleswoman pulled out a crisply folded size 20 from the stack and walked away. My mom handed it to me. In a fleeting moment of appreciation, I almost asked if she still wanted me to go with her for a dress.

Instead, we went to a bookstore and soon returned home with several bags. I showed my dad the items, hiding the boxers as my mom recommended, and thanked him for everything with a kiss on the cheek. His beam of happiness triggered that pit in my stomach, the feeling I tried to repress that our relationship was a sham we were holding on to by the edges of a hundred dollar bill.

My mother kept me company while I packed for my flight the next morning. She sat quietly on my bed, which meant the Q&A session was about to start. I continued to fold the clothes covering my carpet.

"Can I read some of your writing?" she asked.

My mom was loosely aware of the subject matter, that it pertained to my gender and sexuality. "I'm not sure you want to," I replied, grateful that at least she'd asked.

"Do you really want me to go through the recycling bin after you leave?"

I tried not to let my smile out. She was so predictable, which was why I'd packed all of my early drafts to discard at the airport—leaving behind a few random out-of-context pages about testosterone would've been dangerous. "There's nothing in there," I said.

I contemplated giving her my thesis, which I'd decided not to leave with my brother, but even with context, the topics would be hard for her to handle, and I was out of energy, too depleted to even consider helping her through the experience.

"Is that really what you want?" my mom asked. "For me to die without getting to know you?"

Even for my mother, playing the death card was a bit over the top. I pulled the two hundred pages out of the bottom of my backpack. "Here." I skidded the stack across the carpet. It hit the base of my bed. The papers fanned out, held together, just barely, by a clip in the corner.

The one person who did make it through my thesis was Ramona. She read it and responded while I was in Scotland on a trip that might have been fun had I not missed her so much. A couple days in, I discovered what I could only imagine nontraveler types must feel like abroad: far from home, disinterested, and critical. There was no Loch Ness monster, the vegetarian haggis was missing a little something, the men wore skirts, everyone spoke English and yet I couldn't understand a word—all of this would've been fascinating to me if I'd cared about anything besides taking pictures of rock sculptures I built for Ramona. I'd traveled across the country, and then across the ocean, halfway across the world, but everything I wanted was waiting for me in San Francisco. Her response to my thesis came in an e-mail, four words offered after reading sixty thousand of mine, but they were the only ones I needed.

Ramona wrote: "I got your back."

Nine

ROOTS

I hibernated for the winter with Ramona and practiced my boy-friend skills—cuddling, spooning, listening, boning. Without a job to delineate the day of the week, nothing other than rain to separate the months, and a location that only shifted rooms within Ramona's house, everything blended together for me during those nesting months. Even our discussions merged, as if they were part of one large conversation that shaped my boyhood.

It began with a Duraflame log burning in the fireplace, and Ramona lying on the couch with her head in my lap. I could feel her neck tense up as she told me about the argument she'd had with one of our former classmates after helping her move into her new apartment. The whole time, our classmate had made com-ments like, "We need a man for this," which Ramona considered backward thinking from the older woman and feminist she ad-mired. "Then . . . she told me she's not a feminist," Ramona said.

I ran my hand over her strained forehead, debating whether to speak. For an activist, Ramona was not self-righteous, and I counted on her lack of judgment over my moral flaws to give me the room to work through old ways of thinking that I wanted to retire. "I'm not sure I'd call myself a feminist either," I said, ten-tatively.

Ramona shot out of my lap. "What?!" she cried. "How are you not a feminist?!"

"I don't want to be a man-hater," I whined. "And I can't stand people assuming I'm a feminist just because I look like a woman."

I told her about the prochoice fund-raiser for which an A-gay had asked me to read one of my humor essays as part of the entertainment. The money was to fight a restrictive ballot measure calling for parental notification and in her request, my friend implied that even as lesbians, safe from the accidental knock-up, reproductive rights were still "our issue." This was a couple weeks before my pool party breakthrough, and I hadn't acquired the language to express or even understand why I'd been so hurt and offended. I agreed to read at the event even though I wished my friend had meant "our issue" as a society, not "our issue" as women—something that once I could articulate later, I did tell her.

Ramona tugged on her upper lip until I finished. My story must have calmed her down because she spoke in an even, relaxed tone. "Feminism just means political, social, and economic equality for women," she said. "How can anyone be against equality?"

"In that case I'm definitely a feminist," I said, as all of my defensive resistance crumbled. The word that had given me anxiety to utter all of a sudden felt empowering to speak. And it wasn't only Ramona's definition, but my relief in separating myself from women that allowed me to stand behind the cause. I thought of how Jess had said, "Politically, I am a woman." I wasn't, couldn't be, it was too painful to link myself to women with a "to be" verb; it was a matter of semantics, but also identity; I was politically and completely all *for* women.

Over the course of several talks, I admitted everything to Ramona that I'd been too embarrassed, ashamed, and afraid to tell Jess during our kitchen conversations: Until reading transgender books, I had envisioned "social justice" as Judge Wapner from *The People's Court* presiding over a keg party, and I hadn't even heard the term *male privilege* until Jess ranted about it. Jess and Ramona must have at least touched on these subjects in college, where I'd taken almost exclusively science, math, economics, and other precareer path courses.

That was just one of the many excuses and explanations I used for my ignorance. I was also white, raised without any monetary concerns (other than my mom's irrational fears), and American, all of which came with so much privilege heaped upon privilege that I couldn't see out from all my privilege to notice that men could have even more privilege than me. In my family, my parents were equals. I'd grown up believing my mom was as successful, accomplished, and well paid as my dad. But my world view had been very personal, self-involved, and failed to consider institutionalized bias, the systems set up to benefit a specific group, the foundational patriarchy of our culture.

My understanding of male privilege acted as a gateway to exploring all sorts of privileges and how they played into each other, like my extreme class privilege—the advantages too numerous and grand to list—and my cisgender privilege that had been slowly eroding—the privilege to use a restroom without a "wrong bathroom" comment or a call for security, to put on whatever clothes I wanted in the middle of a women's locker room without the harassment of strangers, and to walk the streets outside of an urban center without the threat of being killed for confusing others with my gender variance—the catch-all I'd begun to favor to describe myself for its scientific, almost taxonomical undertone. *Gender fluid* was another amorphous term implying movement, but that one was too hipster for me. Regardless of the identity word of the week, anything outside of *woman* or *man* allowed me to plot myself onto the map of existence. From this point my consciousness could expand.

The concepts Ramona and I discussed were as obvious as water and air to her, but they elicited in me a newfound care for the struggles of all people. It was through the lens of my own otherness that I began to see queerness as something that extended far beyond sexuality and gender, tattoos and dyed hair; for me, it was a state of mind that came with the experience of being the odd, ignored, or devalued one in a society and culture that functioned as if some people's needs were less important than others. It now made sense to me that Ramona had belonged to so many groups on her college campus—the human rights group, the animal rights group, the student rights group, the gay group, and the women's group (which she cofounded)—"our issues" were all connected.

It may have taken me a while to be a feminist on the streets, but even before sex had become a big part of my life, I'd considered myself a feminist in the sheets. In bed, I believed in equal opportunity. If a boy could have a cock, then there was no reason a girl couldn't have one too. Still, Ramona's was a complete surprise. On a dreary, gray afternoon with the rain pattering down on the skylight, she stood in the center of her room and dropped her robe. From her nylon harness, a slender, pink dildo stuck out. It was more like a fashion accessory to match pumps and a bracelet than a penis. "You have a lady dick!" I blurted out.

A deep laugh emerged from her belly. She nodded. "Pretty much. She's called Raquel." Ramona slumped her shoulders, shrinking bashfully, before crawling under the bed covers with me. "I'm not really sure what we're gonna do with her," she said.

"We could sword fight," I replied. "Raquel the Lady Dick versus Isaac the Bandit."

She rolled her eyes. "We're not sword fighting."

It was hot that my girlfriend had a dick, even though cracking jokes was easier than figuring out what to do with her new toy. I considered letting her do me the old-fashioned way, but I envisioned my body as so physically different from hers that to use it in the exact same way would only highlight our similarities. I feared that this would cause me, and maybe her, to see me as a woman. I felt like apologizing for not being an equal opportunist after all. "I'm not sure I can do front hole," I said.

Ramona was silent, her face slack.

"We can at least try," I said. "Or . . ." I rolled over and pushed my ass into her, banging it against her lady dick.

She sighed. I turned to see heaviness settle into her eyes. "What?"

NINA HERE NOR THERE 135

"I don't love *front hole*," she said. "It reminds me of that pamphlet. Those guys were gross."

I'd picked up the term from a safer sex guide at a local gay bar. Most of the people in the pamphlet were very large, very hairy men decked out in leather, the downside of using BDSM material for education. The upside was the respect for the boundaries of trans men, some of whom liked penetration in this "front hole" as long as it was called something that made them comfortable. I admired these guys for transgressing the stereotypical male sex role, connected with their desire to be fucked, and envied them for maximizing their sexual potential. The go-getter in me wanted to enjoy more than just my teeny weeny. Here I had the coolest body part imaginable, a hole that delivered orgasms and babies—it seemed like such a waste to squander it, and a failing on my part to let the stifling framework of gender win, when holes and poles didn't always have to be so loaded, and could just be erogenous zones.

A term like *front hole* was my only chance to enforce the physical distinction I felt to women, to ungender my anatomy. "I don't know what else to say." I looked directly into Ramona's eyes, pleading. She inched closer. Through my T-shirt, I felt her nipples bristle against mine. I backed away, but the sensation lingered, expanded until all I could feel was the weight of my chest. I quickly flipped from my side to my back. "I don't know what to do anymore."

Ramona nodded, understanding. She always did. But even her support, even the power of language to rechart the landscape of my body and the amazing breadth of my expanding lexicon to identify myself turned flimsy in the reflection of the concrete. A few weeks later, while Ramona and I were kissing in front of the mirrored doors of her closet, I caught sight of myself in full and noticed the subtle round of my outer thighs as they tapered to my hips. I stopped kissing her and faced the mirror. "My legs are so girly," I said.

She busted out laughing. "Your legs are not girly," she said.

It didn't matter that my legs were the least feminine part of my entire body. "That's what I look like?" I asked.

She stared at me as if this were a trick question.

Even with clothes covering me, there was no mistaking the shapely lines underneath. My sports bra was too loose, my boxer briefs too tight. I dropped to the carpet and crossed my legs. In the past year, I'd scrutinized my reflection hundreds of times, but always alone. I'd never imagined what another person, what Ramona took in while we messed around. "You see a girl when you look at me," I accused.

She leaned forward and kissed me softly on the cheek, then the lips.

"I can't believe you see a girl." I picked myself off the floor and climbed into her bed, tucking my knees into my chest.

She followed and curled around me, speaking quietly into my ear. "I don't see girl or not girl when I look at you. You know I think of you as a person. You're just Nina to me." She paused. "Although I'd never call you that in bed."

For the first time, I noticed the complete absence of my name during sex. Had Ramona ever used it, I probably would've been alarmed; I didn't feel like a "Nina" during sexy time. But what else could she have called me? My alter ego, Nick, stayed silent; my role-play characters had names, like Timmy and Dirk, but those only worked if I was playing a middle school student or faggy frat boy; and of course, there was Isaac. I, as myself, went nameless.

"I'd never thought about 'Nina' like that before. I'm glad you don't say it." Hearing my name would've been as jarring as catching my reflection in the mirror. Now that I saw with vivid clarity what I looked like in Ramona's presence, I feared that her compliments, any flattering remark about my physical appearance, would be an insult, her attraction to me disparaging. "I realize I can't control what about my body turns you on," I continued, keeping my back to her as I spoke. "But don't ever talk about it. I can never know."

By the end of the winter, my job search was the same as it had been at the beginning of the winter. It consisted of me reading but not applying for uninspiring job listings online, sending a few networking e-mails, and refreshing my e-mail in case an opportunity fell into my inbox. I kept myself somewhat occupied, volunteering, interning, writing, and occasionally jogging or snowboarding, but I felt purposeless and stuck. I kept turning to Ramona for motivation; I wanted her to get us to do something, anything other than fucking, sleeping, or eating. We talked constantly about spending more time apart, pursuing our own interests, but the last time I'd engaged in regular social and sports activities was before grad school and it was like I'd forgotten how. Even when her bed felt like a quagmire, I stayed, driven more by my fear of being without her than the joy I had once taken in being with her.

At my home, a place where I spent about one night a week regrouping, Melissa gave a month's notice and packed up within days, having already signed the lease on a new place with her girlfriend. I sat on the steps that led down to her empty room as she swept it for the final time, our voices echoing off the bare walls as we talked. She told me she hoped to become close with Jess again once they were no longer living together. "I don't know what's going on with him," she said. "He's talking about having top surgery as if it's the answer to everything." Shocked by her statement, I tried to pry more out, but she only said Jess and his long-distance girlfriend were maybe ending things—again. Melissa might as well have been talking gibberish. I was so far removed from what went on in my house, I'd had no idea Melissa and Jess weren't getting along, much less that Jess was seriously considering top surgery.

Ramona and I had a very pragmatic discussion about the vacancy at my house. She was sick of roommates who built dirty-dish castles in the sink, and I was sick of living out of a bag on her floor, so while we understood that we were responding to circumstances, we also agreed that an opportunity for her to move in had presented itself. We joined forces in excitement over sharing two rooms, a bedroom and an office, and turned all talk to a creative brainstorm about design layouts, wall decorations, and furniture shopping sprees.

A week later, however, once our fantasy rooms jelled into impending reality, I woke up in the middle of the night at her house in a panic. All that I'd repressed from the day we got together resurfaced and fed into my certainty that our relationship wasn't for the long term. Perhaps we could've remained in our holding pattern, but my personal stagnancy, my need for some change, any shift, prompted me to be honest and tell her that I couldn't ever see myself living with her.

Once I spoke, Ramona suggested we take some space, which we were only able to maintain for forty-eight hours before agreeing we weren't ready to breakup. It had all happened so quickly, too quickly to split up. But from that point forward, we both knew it was only a matter of time, of resigning ourselves, and this impacted every aspect of our relationship. She'd always been a night owl to my early bird, and now we started to go to bed at different times; we lost patience with each other in our debates over books, current events, and animal rights; we stopped meeting halfway on everything. For two months we had constant fights, most of which I picked but can't remember because they all fell under the broader, "I want you to be someone you're not" fight, or the "Why can't you do something so this doesn't have to end" fight.

Our last fight occurred on a Saturday in April. Ramona wanted to hang out after her crappy workday, and I'd reached the maximum number of nights I could spend on her couch watching TV. We fell easily into a conversation about breaking up, one that we continued for the next week, in person and on the phone, until it became too depressing and painful to drag on. We agreed it would be best to cut off contact indefinitely, our eventual friendship the goal. I offered to do the exchange of property while Ramona was at work, volunteering only because I'd made an appointment with my old therapist, whom I hadn't seen in a year, to comfort me afterward.

I used my key to enter Ramona's front door, the same key she'd asked me to leave behind so she wouldn't wait, wishing for my return. I trudged up the long, carpeted stairway. In her room, the finality hit me immediately. The one framed picture of us, my gift for her recent twenty-fourth birthday, had been removed from the wall, and her bed, squeezed into a new location in the corner after we'd decided not to live together, looked all wrong—so far from the window we used to open to pretend we were outside.

In the center of her carpet, a brown paper bag and cardboard box held some of my clothes, biking and snowboarding gear, and Isaac. My yellow auto mechanic T-shirt, the one she'd worn the very first time she slept over at my house, was missing—she'd called it her "boyfriend" shirt—I hoped she'd kept it intentionally. On top of the pile, a red Post-it Note grabbed my attention. The large black lettering read: "I'm grateful for having had the chance to love you." Before I even noticed, a few drops had fallen from my eyes, splattering big wet splotches onto her note. The grace of her words, her sense of appreciation during this hard time, encompassed everything that had drawn me to her, all that I was devastated to lose.

I took one final look around the room, out the window at the flowers on the bougainvillea tree, at the titles on her bookshelf from the classes we'd taken together, and into the corner, empty without my belongings piled there. I removed her key from my chain and wrapped my hand around it, squeezing tightly, holding on for as long as I could. "Good-bye," I said aloud, as if signifying the end could make it easier to let go.

It was in retrospect that I realized the challenge of opening up to physical and emotional intimacy was nothing compared to the experience of losing it. At no other time than in the few weeks after the end of our relationship did I live with such a constant struggle for peace from the internal soundtrack of disappointment, sadness, and emptiness. I went on "what if" tears in my head and to my friends, stating everything I could do differently, as if there might be a way for the situation to change, for Ramona and I to get back together, for me to stop missing her. But the only thing harder than what I was going through would've been to call or connect with her and have to go through our separation again.

A former coworker recommended me for a copywriting job at a travel dot-com, a blessing if only because my cubicle provided the one place I couldn't cry. Unable to sit still outside of work, I traded my daily writing practice for jogs in the park, spin classes, and long bike rides, as if I could expel all my emotions through the physical release of sweating. Perpetually lonely, I said "yes" to any and all social invites with a mix of people too broad to unite under one category. My friends included a few individual A-gays; an old pal, Sandra, whom I hadn't seen in several years, but bumped into at the gym and reconnected with instantly; and my new roommate, Derek, whom I was getting to know now that I'd returned home permanently after my year on the love planet.

Referred by an A-gay who'd received my mass e-mail about the vacancy, Derek was a rugged, incredibly attractive gym-rat with B-cup pecs and the most wonderfully sweet smile. In his first week in the house, without any instruction, he added his high school picture to our refrigerator, the first cis guy to contribute to our growing living document. As it turned out, Derek had had twice as much hair at eighteen, proving my theory that man, woman, or other—none of us were the same people we once were. To post his picture he used his own magnet, which said in huge letters, "I ♥ My Penis."

Once Derek joined Jess and me, what had felt like a dyke house when I moved in two and a half years before was now a dude home, and a sort of sad bachelor pad at that. With all three of us recovering from breakups, Derek dubbed our apartment Heartbreak Hotel, and he granted us all a temporary moratorium on sanity. For him, this meant swearing off sex. For Jess, it meant marathon processing phone calls with his ex with intermission dinner breaks at the three-hour mark. And for me, it meant stalking Ramona's MySpace page, public to even those like myself without a profile.

Which is what I was doing on a Sunday morning, three weeks after our breakup, when I discovered Ramona's mind-in-the-gutter headline and comments from friends like, "What happened last night?" and "Are you coming home?" Certain that she'd met someone, or at least had a fling, I hopped on the crazy train to obsessionville. Who was this person? Girl or boy? Did gender matter? Was she over me? Did our relationship mean nothing? That's how Jess found me, circling the kitchen in my pajamas, spinning in my web of self-destruction. "Maybe you should take a walk," Jess said in a manner so calm I felt even more frenzied.

I nodded my head aggressively. "Good idea, good idea," I repeated. "Good idea."

"And when you get back, you should come to yoga with me and Greg!"

I paced around the neighborhood for the next hour, and then, with no other options besides internal combustion, I walked with Jess over to the yoga studio a few blocks from our house. I had been there for the first time the previous Friday, a night not all that different from this morning, except instead of going with a friend from grad school who was like a contortionist, I now had the comforting companionship of other beginners, radiating their contagious excitement. "Quick, come next to me," Greg said as we filed into the steamy, barn-size studio.

Instantaneously surrounded by well over a hundred mats, laid out in columns and rows inches apart, Jess, Greg, and I sat in a line. Having exchanged only basic pleasantries in the past year, Greg and I caught up among the cacophony of friendly chatter. He told me he was sorry about my breakup, and when I asked how he was doing, he responded with a complete update on his body —the expansion of his head and neck, the thickening of his chest, his decreased flexibility, which he showed me by attempting some around-the-back arm wrap. Greg was built like a beer can, not quite what I expected to see in yoga class, but then again, neither was Jess, with his personality more suited to say "Fuck downward dog" than to do one.

If I wondered what they were doing in that studio, the easy answer was the teacher, Rusty, whom they raved about. He strolled in fifteen minutes late, wearing only a pair of short swim trunks that showed off his tan, lean, and rippled figure. He immediately launched the class into a melodic chant, the Sanskrit words too complicated for me to follow, and then, with an energy that was both ecstatic and sustainable, disarming and motivational, he led us through basic poses, throwing in breath cues, inspirational wisdom, and encouragement.

Forget the cobra and warrior poses, I could barely stand on one foot and act like a tree. I kept expecting my high school basketball coach to appear at the door yelling, "You lost, Krieger? Tip-off's in five minutes." And when I wasn't thinking about Ramona sleeping in someone else's bed, I was thinking of how much coffee I drank. Finally, I got tired of thinking about how badly I had to pee, so I went to the bathroom. Once there I was compelled, as always, to fixate on my reflection in the mirror.

My tight tank top scooped low enough that even with a Frog Bra underneath, I was baring cleavage. For a second, I felt like I'd been caught illegally without a binder, and that a doctor or lawyer could pull out footage later and point to this as evidence that I'd been faking my chest discomfort. I briefly wondered what Jess and Greg, both in T-shirts, thought about my outfit, and I found myself relieved not to care. From just my one Friday night yoga class, I already felt this studio was a safe space to let go of self-consciousness, to moo like a cow and shake my ass while sitting in an invisible chair. I returned to class, eager to forget what my body looked like and experience the sensations of being inside of it.

But it was hard to feel when I was so busy checking out Jess, Greg, and everyone around me, trying to morph my body into poses that looked like theirs. As if busting me, Rusty would say, "If you don't know what to do, watch your neighbor, do what they do." At first I couldn't tell if he was joking, but I was pretty sure he was trying to tell me that someone else's body, someone else's experience would not show me how to have mine.

I followed the instructions as well as I could to root my mountain into the ground, breath deeply into my pigeon, and rock myself peacefully in happy baby. Somewhere along the way, my pinky toes woke up, my jaw and shoulders relaxed, and a power emerged from my core. By the end of it all, I was drenched in sweat, lying on my back, my legs and arms slack, my whole body exhausted but alive. Although thoughts of Ramona fluttered back in during this final resting pose, I recognized there'd been a whole half hour when I didn't think of her once, when my dialogue of despair disappeared. I was feeling so good that I sang along in the last chant, a repetition of only a few words. I felt even better when I discovered that it loosely translated to, "May all beings everywhere be happy and free."

On the street, Greg said good-bye, mimicking Rusty. "Don't roll up the yoga when you roll up the mat." Jess laughed, his eyes aglow. Sunday mornings with Rusty became our ritual.

With yoga, I had an activity in common with Greg, and now if I spotted him across the dyke bar that wasn't completely a dyke bar, we'd nearly run to each other, ignoring any cute girls, and talk yoga. We'd discuss challenging poses, deliver a play-by-play if one of us missed a class and brag if Rusty had touched and adjusted us or whispered something encouraging. At home, Jess and I took our practice further, exchanging alignment tips and sharing breakthrough moments with the same enthusiasm we'd once discussed gender, but without the hard edge, as if we were flushing out our previous anger, frustration, and confusion with each kitchen vinyasa. Although Jess, Greg, and I didn't consider ourselves gay, we were all gay for Rusty. He was our bond, an expression of all the individual work we were doing together.

The basics class was an entertaining, music-infused workout

so challenging it focused me away from my thoughts, but it was more than exercise. The ancient philosophical teachings mixed with aphorisms to come out as Rusty-isms, and they lodged themselves into the new space inside of me. "Yoga is a process of undoing," he'd say. On my mat, I was unlearning a lifetime of survival habits, building strength to carry myself, creating a foundation to raise my community, remaining present in moments of intense discomfort, staying still when all I wanted to do was flee.

I'd thought I was going to that studio to move on from Ramona and the relationship I'd entered on the cusp of my boyhood, but as I returned week after week, I found myself mourning for my own former self, letting go of my attachment to an unquestioned, recognized, accepted gender. What I thought and expected my life to be, being a woman—all of it was gone. There was no distraction, plan of attack, work-around or escape, nowhere to go, nothing I could do but breathe.

I always went to the bathroom early in the class and looked at myself, unable to remember the time before every mirror stole my attention. As my practice of yoga led me to connect more with feelings inside my body, the distance to my reflection increased until all I could see in my tank top was a stranger with breasts staring back at me. Each time I'd ask myself, Can you live like this? The more classes I attended in a week, the more visits I made to the bathroom. My obsession with my self-image had grown so strong, it was no longer my chest I was referring to, but my endless focus on my reflection, my extreme searching for something intangible, when I asked: Can you live like this?

My greatest fear after my breakup was that I'd revert to being an intimacy-phobe, unable to maintain a steady physical relationship with anyone for another seven years. But now that I had a new vocabulary to express and understand myself, getting involved with women was easy once I put down my Deepak Chopra to look for them. About two months out, I found an alternative online dating site and attempted to write a profile worthy of virtual flowers that explained without invoking gender theory that I was neither woman nor man, but rather a dude prone to bad PMS.

Through this site, I ended up going out with just one person, Linda, an intelligent, attractive uber-Jew who unfortunately talked more than my mother. We dated for three weeks, and her words upon our split, that perhaps I was only looking for post breakup sex, were, in hindsight, entirely accurate. We slept together enough times for me to prove how comfortable I was with my physical discomfort. I was able to tell Linda how to touch and talk about my body, a skill that I now realized was called "communication" and was rather useful, regardless of a person's gender.

Although binding was newish to Linda, in the periphery of her awareness, from my profile she had at least some sense of what she was getting into with me, whereas Jill, a writer I met through a friend, did not. Jill sent me frustrating texts like, "Girl, you've got it going on." I told her that girl words were a no-no, as was using "Nina" while fucking, which she accidentally did once, the first time my name truly upset me. Startled by the name that called up an image and identity so far from my current, crucial self-perception, I shut down completely, my connection to my body and to her lost as I reflexively reverted to my old autopilot mode. It took three weeks of awkward moments and explanatory conversations for Jill to see me as I saw myself, and it was a bittersweet end when she said it had taken her a long time to be comfortable, proud, and out as a lesbian and she didn't want to date a guy.

Single and slutting about the city, I wore my binder everywhere. Having it on was a matter of personal confidence, but it also served as a clue, a litmus test, or a segue into the public service announcement portion of a hookup. I had no idea what my binder would elicit when I took Tessa, a plain yet pretty brunette, home from a lesbian party. We'd been making out in my bed for a while, her shirt and bra off, when I told her I was wearing too many layers. In front of my dresser, I removed my long-sleeved shirt and the T-shirt on over it. Then, I grasped my binder from the bottom and stripped it off. I inhaled deeper than I had all day, letting my lungs fully expand, forgetting for a moment that Tessa was there.

"Why do you wear that?" she whispered.

"I'm just not comfortable having breasts," I replied, relieved to see her understanding nod, a sweetness that hadn't emerged in our shallow flirtations.

In a fresh T-shirt, I got back into bed, and from my position underneath her, on my back where gravity worked its flattening magic, my shirt started to slip up above my belly button. I let it go, riding up, wanting to feel her skin against mine. When Tessa noticed my rising shirt, her entire face turned sympathetic. I considered telling her about the rulebook—there were ways to make my chest work, I just couldn't move, or watch, or do anything that might cause me to notice my breasts. But with her compassionate eyes lingering upon me, I wanted to burn the rulebook. As Tessa gently tugged my shirt back down, I heard an answer to my all-consuming question. I probably could live like this, but why was I fighting so hard to?

Ten

THE GOOD-BYE WAD

By the time September rolled around, I was finally feeling stable and solid after my breakup, mentally and physically grounded from four months of yoga, running, a steady paycheck, and the support group that was our home at Heartbreak Hotel. I also had some bonus confidence from my newfound success with casual dating. The San Francisco summer hit right on schedule, bringing blue skies, sun, and the few nights a year with temperatures high enough to wear shorts. If ever a time was perfect for my parents to visit me, this was it.

And I had been waiting for almost nine years; their one visit during that stretch was the previous December, a mere forty-eight-hour stopover on their way home from Palm Springs. My mom had come to San Francisco a few times alone, and although the reasons for my dad's absences went undiscussed between me and him, I considered it part of our "Don't Ask, Don't Tell" policy, extended to include my home city, my home, all of me and my life. In the one conversation I'd had with my mom about their lack of visits, she'd claimed that San Francisco wasn't a top vacation destination for them—why come to me when they could ski in Jackson Hole or golf in Bermuda? I wanted to believe my mom, and had some reason to, because when they flew through in December and recognized the possibilities for fun presented by Zagat's and wine country, they immediately planned this big trip for the following fall, a full week, including a few days in Calistoga.

With constant noise, mindless chatter, and perpetual mother-daughter bickering, seven days was the anxiety-provoking equivalent of seven dog years with my parents. I counted on the refuge of my work cubicle for a couple days, and the assistance of my relatives. My dad's first cousin, Sherri, lived in a beautiful apartment with a panoramic view of both bridges, where my parents would stay, and her "separated-but-on-amicable-terms" husband, Ted, would help entertain them. Recent transplants from Arizona, Ted and Sherri were another draw for my parents. It was a coincidence that their daughter Perry—an older cousin I'd met only three times before—and her husband were hosting a Jewish naming ceremony for their newborn, or what I thought of as a girl version of a bris, on the afternoon of my parents' arrival.

I met my parents at Perry's house, in the hills not far from my own home, and spotted them hunched over the spread of catered Middle Eastern food. It had been nine months since I'd last seen them, and even from across the room they appeared to have aged, or at least looked their age, early sixties, reminding me of my brother's last-minute survival advice: think of them as cute old people, an elderly couple, someone else's grandparents. Between the lines I heard: just let them be.

When my mom saw me, she broke into a smile so explosive, it nearly launched off her face. She hugged me before my dad opened his arms and I slipped into the padded pocket of his body. Pulling back, he held me with his eyes, buoyant with love. The intensity was too much, like staring at the sun. I glanced away, missing the flash of change, but my eyes returned to find his eyebrows crested into flints of concern, his cheeks bulging with fire. A shudder of terror ran through me. "Did you have an operation?!" he said.

I quickly scanned the room. We were surrounded by people, relatives, the safety of others; he couldn't make a scene. I relaxed a notch, came back to myself, to him, and noticed the harsh glare of his eyes locked on my binder-flattened chest.

"No, no. They're, um . . ." I stuttered in shock. My dad couldn't know about top surgery, could he? "You can't see. But they're there," I continued to stumble, my tone placating. His cheeks relaxed and the heat drained from his eyes. "They're there," I reiterated. "I lost some weight."

My mom stepped forward, the effort to recover her joyful smile apparent. "You look great, honey."

I was still reeling inside. I knew my clothes were significantly baggier, but I'd had no idea my appearance had changed so dramatically.

"The thinnest you've ever looked," my mom said. "Even here." She grabbed my love handles. "Staying away from those bagels?"

"Nope," I said. "Just exercising."

She wanted to know how much weight I'd lost. Uncertain myself, I refused to tell my mother, who in the heat of a fight once dared me to be anorexic, my guess of ten to fifteen pounds.

My dad caressed my cheek with the back of his hand. I forced out a kind smile in return before escaping to the bar, a card table covered with a white tablecloth. I scanned the ice buckets for hard booze to calm the blood careening through my veins, but it was a beer and wine affair. I went with the red.

The caterer cocked her head. "Are you old enough to drink, young man?"

"Old enough and then some," I replied.

She poured my drink without hesitation, and without the usual "sorry, ma'am" apology, typical once I revealed the pitch of my voice. Now, I wondered how much I had changed, if it was more than dropping weight. I thought back to my brief get-together with Zippy the previous month, after a separation too long to quantify. While complimenting me on my slimmer appearance, she'd alluded to something deeper. She said it was as if I was willing my chest away.

Whether external or internal, something had shifted enough to make my father believe I'd had an "operation." He must have meant a "sex-change operation"—a term I considered obsolete and misleading. But sex-change operation or top surgery, I was now certain of what I'd suspected, that after all the disappointments I'd handed my father over the years, nothing would be worse than a flat-chested daughter. I drank half my glass of wine in two gulps.

When I returned to my parents, they were talking to Sherri, a good-natured, glamorous woman who along with her sister had grown up on the same apartment floor as my dad's family, sharing a party line with my dad and his sister. This was back on the Lower East Side, where money was scarce, city college was the only option, and the goal was to end up better off than their parents— a raging success all around, so much so that when my dad once drove me past what had been my grandfather's jewelry store, I had a hard time comprehending the burnt out Krieger sign as a root to my life. From my birth, the only real questions were whether to start me with tennis or squash, piano or saxophone, and which Ivy League school I'd eventually attend.

Sherri greeted me warmly, same as she had two years before when I arrived at her house for dinner and we'd first reconnected. "Nice to meet you," Sherri had said, humorously acknowledging fifteen years without a major family event to bring us together. A reunion of sorts, the special occasion was Robin, my dad's sister, in town for a visit. Over brisket and brussels sprouts I listened quietly as the adults (which I still considered them to be, even though I was now one too) reminisced about their childhood. They gushed over my dad, praising his protection and care of them as young girls, claiming *everybody* loved him, which was still true. His kindness and charisma were his most defining traits, and I'd inherited all of mine from him.

Despite the dripping nostalgic sentiment, hearing about my dad, his humbleness, generosity, and his past, a subject he rarely touched aside from his mother's multiple sclerosis, caused me to tear up at the dinner table. Moved by the greatness of my father, my rush of affection seeped into a deep sadness over the skeleton of our relationship, the gay obstacle we'd never overcome.

In recent years, I'd tried to convince myself that his initial devastation must have passed, that I was holding on too tight to comments he'd made when I was in my early twenties, like, "I can love you without loving everything about you." But Robin had brought her first girlfriend to that reunion dinner, their serious lesbian relationship something my dad had completely failed to mention to me. That night, Robin told me that in our entire family, my dad was the only one who wasn't entirely supportive of her relationship—she didn't know why. Once his sister couldn't elicit a sense of acceptance from him, I gave up hoping he'd moved forward, or believing he was capable of it.

At the front of the living room, the ceremony began. With her husband and rabbi beside her, Perry held the baby girl. I disconnected once the *Baruch Atta Adonai* business started, my heritage still something that made me uneasy. Far from religious, my immediate family read the Chanukah blessings off the candle box, and I'd memorized my haftarah from an audio tape to have a bat mitzvah only because I wanted to be like all the other kids in my private NYC school and summer camp.

I'd been shaped by a cultural Judaism, defined by obnoxiously extravagant parties for thirteen-year-olds, pressure to reach a very high bar of achievement, skiing on Christmas Day, and the regular sounds of a few lawyers engaged in an intellectual circle jerk about the Way Things Are. And I will never forget the stories and images of mass graves, crematoriums, and gas chambers, shown and told to me at an age *way* too young to know about such horrors. As I grew older, I found it unsettling that the adults who had burnt the plight of our ancestors into me appeared to have such myopia that they couldn't see, or care enough as I wanted them to, that people other than Jews suffered, that discrimination and violence against many groups, including gays like me, still happened all the time.

I focused on the sleeping baby girl and imagined all of the expectations the people in this room would saddle her with, or those she'd place upon herself, the difference between the two in my own life now imperceptible to me—it had started so early, without a ceremony but with my name. I was named after Norman, my mother's only sibling, hit by a car and killed on his way to dinner with his wife, the incident that incited my conception a couple months later. In the story I told myself about who my mother was, how she came to be, it was first the loss of her father, an unhealthy gambling man who had a heart attack at the race track when she was in college, and then her older brother, a legendary basketball player and her hero, gone when she was my age, thirty, that had made a lonely, fighting survivor out of her.

I received my middle name, "Beth," from my paternal grandmother, Belle, who passed away shortly before I was born. The story I held on to about my father was built around his mother and his childhood lost, caring for her, pushing her wheelchair, feeding and carrying her as she slowly degenerated from multiple sclerosis.

Often Jews pass on only the first letter in the names of the dead, and I held the honor of my relatives in the N and B, even though what was buried inside them went to my core. In the story I created about myself, I'd been born out of the greatest traumas of my parents' lives, as if their tragedies had been built into my constitution, and my purpose on this earth was to save them from grief and loss.

The rest of the San Francisco portion of my parents' visit went smoothly. The true test came with the challenge of confined spaces, our three-day trip to Calistoga. Sherri lent us her Lexus hardtop convertible, which had a backseat made for airplane carry-on luggage, not a human being like myself. It was too small for three people but asking my parents to pay for a rental car when offered a free black sports car would've been incomprehensible. If they'd asked me to get in the trunk and promised breathing holes, I would've obliged. It might've been more comfortable.

After three spine-destroying hours, we arrived at our resort, where our room was a freestanding cottage with a patio of wicker furniture, beach cruiser bikes parked in front, and views of the mountains. My dad disappeared with a Denis Johnson novel, and my mom grabbed my hand to explore the resort village and spa facilities. On our tour, she enthusiastically rated each amenity—showers constructed of exotic stones, eucalyptus-scented steam rooms, cucumber-infused water—as "good," "bad," or "stupid" features. It was entertaining and easy to be around my mom when she focused her judgment on something other than me, and although I could care less whether a shower had one or eleven showerheads, I enjoyed sharing her excitement.

We made our dinner reservations through the concierge, who also provided me with a four-mile jogging route. Back in the room, I pulled my running shorts and sports bra out of my ripped athletic bag, conscious of the rare silence. My mom sat on the edge of the bed, picking at the skin around her thumb. "What's the thing you wear underneath your shirt?" she asked.

I hovered above my bag, not at all surprised by her question, only that she'd dug into the Q&A so soon after our arrival. "It's called a binder," I said.

"You wear it to look flat?" Her tone was nonconfrontational, fearful rather than defensive.

I wished I hadn't given her my thesis last year, felt guilty about leaving her with material clearly too painful for her to get through alone. But now that I was more secure, certain that for as long as I had breasts I would have binders, I could either start educating my mom or face perpetual inquisition.

"Yes," I said, and turning on my sweetest pedagogic voice, I added, "Do you want to see it?"

She shook her head weakly. "No, honey, I don't think so."

I carried my running clothes into the marble bathroom and changed over the cushioned bench. When I returned, my mom was still perched on the edge of the bed. "Why do you want to look flat?" she asked, her curiosity palpable.

"It makes me feel more comfortable."

She stared into her lap, focused on her interlocked fingers, a trick we both used to avoid picking. "Where do you get them?"

"A website." I leaned down to put the jeans and binder I'd removed back into my bag. "Are you sure you don't want to see? I can show it to you." I took her lack of response as an indication to continue. "It's just a tank top," I said. I pulled the binder from my bag and held it up. "See, it's like a stretchy tank top."

"It's kind of like a girdle." She sounded relieved.

"Yeah. Totally. I guess you could say that." I felt accomplished, like I'd just shown a kid that there were no monsters under her bed, but before I could rejoice, my mom returned to her usual self. "Most women would do anything for a larger chest and my daughter wants a smaller one," she complained.

And what is so bad about that, I wanted to say. But instead of launching a fight, I strapped my iPod to my shoulder and put in my earphones. Once out the door, I started to jog. I picked up my pace to get out of the resort, onto a side road bordering a vineyard. I ran hard until I was sweating and could no longer think about anything, even my chest, the weight that all my exercise could never shed.

The next morning, my mother introduced me to Pilates reformer machines, contraptions that used elastic bands for resistance, and we sat side by side, following an instructor in strength-building exercises. My mom threw the same maniacal energy into her workouts as she did her jabbering, and, a lifelong athlete, she was now a senior-citizen jock, a physical specimen of lean muscle, an inspiration. After class, I had a massage, a treat my parents often successfully dangled before me so I'd join them on their luxury trips. At night, we ate at a sushi restaurant, pounding the pieces of nigiri and sashimi as if they were potato chips, while we took turns being the butt of each other's jokes.

For the next two days we continued the merriment of a typical Krieger vacation. Always a little oblivious in our fancy surroundings, at wineries we stuck our noses too far into the wine glasses, and in restaurants we donned makeshift napkin bibs to protect from the dangers of sauce spray. On bike rides to town, my mom and I sped ahead of my dad, trash talking as we passed him. When my dad and I needed a break from my mom verbalizing all her thoughts, we sat on the wicker furniture outside the cottage and read.

On Friday, our last day, I snuck out in the morning for an early jog. I followed a quiet road, the mountains around me socked in by a dense fog that lifted as I ran through the valley. It was hot by the time I returned to the room, where my parents had left me a note. I changed into my bathing suit and T-shirt and found them in the pool, surrounded by dozens of chaise lounges, all empty but theirs. The grounds were deserted, the atmosphere so tranquil I could hear every droplet of water land, each splash, from where I sat, watching them in the shallow end.

My dad dipped underwater, letting my mom climb onto his back and hook her hands around his shoulders. He pushed off the wall, propelling them forward, the ruffles on her skirt rippling as he tugged her along with a strong breaststroke. After a few seconds, he rose enough for her head to break the surface, and she took in air through her gaping smile. He remained underwater for the length of the pool, holding his breath, a skill he'd developed as a high school swimmer. At the far wall, my mom requested "again," prodding him into another aquatic donkey ride.

I couldn't believe my eyes. My parents had a private game, a couple activity. I thought back to the times when their divorce seemed like an imminent possibility. My father would storm around, his eyes a squinty torrent of rage as he ranted about how some decision I'd made would ruin my life. Like a husband who blames his wife for not producing a son, my dad seemed to blame my mom for my inability to meet his expectations. But once I left the house, their relationship improved. Now, attached to each other in the pool like two wizened turtles silently copulating, their behavior even seemed eerily romantic. There was happiness between them, independent of me. Perhaps it had been there all along, and I'd been too consumed by my own guilt to notice.

Soon, my dad was standing by my side, dripping onto the concrete, drying himself with a large towel. He reached over for the business section of the *New York Times*. His eyes lingered on my legs. "You don't shave anymore?"

The golf cap he'd donned was so doofy, his bushy eyebrows a mess. I tried to invoke my brother's advice. Just let Dad be, I told myself. But there was disdain in his question, the same one he'd asked me last year, and we'd already been through, "You don't wear earrings anymore?" the year before, and "Are you ever going to grow your hair again?" the year before that. I couldn't let him be. I wasn't my brother. My dad wanted different answers to the questions he asked my brother about his job or activity choices; he wanted a different answer from me as to how I expressed myself as a person. "It sure looks like I don't shave," I said.

Just then my mom stuck her head, hair askew, red goggle rings around her eyes, over the edge of the pool, and I jumped at her invitation to leave my dad for the hot tub. Five minutes later, after my mom and I had both escaped from the near boiling water to sit on the ledge, I could feel her eyes on my faded black Frog Bra. I braced myself for round two of bonding time. "How come you don't wear a bathing suit?" my mom asked.

"I am wearing a bathing suit," I said.

"A real bathing suit?"

"It is real. These are boy's swim trunks." If I hadn't loved the sun on my bare skin, I would've worn a wetsuit to the pool. "How come your bathing suit has ruffles?"

"It's what old people wear."

Steam floated up off the water, clouding the air between us.

"Do you want to be a boy?" she asked.

We had been building toward this very moment from the near catastrophe upon my parents' arrival. I was relieved she had brought the issue into the open, at least between the two of us. But what could I say? My mom didn't understand the words and identities I'd uncovered—genderqueer, gender variant, gender fluid, trans-masculine—nothing existed to her between or beyond girl and boy, and I didn't fully relate to either anymore. I thought to tell her about my body, that right then I could feel an energetic sensation in my chest, as if my breasts were lifting off of me, like helium balloons trying to float away. But I was reminded of Jess, the very first time he'd said he felt "disconnected" to his tits, how ludicrous that sounded. I went with the simplest answer in my arsenal, making the only distinction she might possibly understand, that between experience and self-image. "It's not that I want to be a boy. It's that when I look in the mirror, I expect to see a boy," I said.

"Yeah, well, when I look in the mirror I expect to see less wrinkles and smaller thighs." She focused on the gurgling water, the tiny torrential eddies. "I don't understand. I just don't understand."

Had I not lived in my own body every second of every day, my answer would not have made sense to me either. "Mom, you and I are different people. You don't have to understand."

She wiped the hair out of her face and the guns of her biceps flared. Through her bathing suit, I could see the six-pack of her abs, taut as guitar strings, the strength that she used to muscle through that which defied force. "But I want to understand," she said.

I reminded her that she once couldn't understand me being gay. She dismissed the point, said that wasn't a big deal. But it had been huge. The only reason we could have this conversation now was because both of us had grown in the past ten years, over these long slow bonding sessions that always depleted the last reserves of my patience, which hit empty this time when she asked if I was the boy in a gay relationship.

"If anything, I'm *a* boy, not *the* boy," I said, failing to elaborate that this would make any relationship with a girl not gay at all. Now, if I were to get with a boy, that would be very, very gay. But explaining my existence in her absolute terms was impossible. I called the conversation quits and left for the steam room, where she let me be alone, safe from her scrutiny.

On the drive back to San Francisco, we visited a few more wineries. At each stop, I climbed out of the backseat, watched my mom pound her samples, passed on my own to avoid a midday buzz that would only leave me sleepy and cranky, and crammed myself back into the pod again. My mom claimed tastings didn't make her feel "high," her word for intoxicated, but by the time we'd made it out of wine country, she was talking in double time without pause.

"Your friend we met the other night, Sandra," my mom said. "She has a lot of tattoos."

"And?" I replied, stretching out my cramped legs sideways on the seat next to me.

"And I guess I don't understand why anyone would do that."

I rolled down the small piece of glass that passed for my window. The air outside was as stale and hot as the air inside. We were barely moving, stuck in traffic. "I like her tattoos," I said.

"Sandra was very nice," my mom said. "I guess I'm just wondering if you have any normal friends?"

Anticipating the fight neither of us had the energy for, I flipped around in my seat, fidgeting for an out. The leather back, ramrod and stiff, pressed into my spinal column, closing in like a medieval death chamber. "What does that mean?" I asked.

"I don't know, people with similar values."

"You mean values like compassion, kindness, empathy?" I said to the back of her head.

My mother craned her neck to face me. "Just people like us."

"Like us?"

"You know, that do things like us."

As I obnoxiously brought up my one friend who played golf, the GPS, in the voice of a female robot, announced the directions for our next turn. My dad veered off the congested main road and cut underneath the highway. The GPS instructed us to turn right. I saw a closed on-ramp on the right. My internal voice of caution instructed me to abort the conversation. "What does that even mean, normal?" I asked. "White, straight, no visible tattoos or piercings?"

"Why did you ask, if you know what I mean?" my mom snapped.

Because I needed to be one hundred percent sure that everything I'd once aspired to be was based on your definition, not mine, I thought, before I spouted off names, listing my friends along with their marks of shame—eyebrow ring, shoulder tattoo, black, Latina, bisexual. Even my friends who fit her bill had some weird-ass habits, like buying ancient medical devices on eBay or making gory movies by bloodying children's dolls. "*Who* is normal?" I asked.

My dad, following the directions on the GPS, circled back around to the same closed on-ramp.

"I guess I was just thinking of your brother's friends," my mom said.

His friends were athletic, attractive, intelligent white guys. They reminded me of my A-gays and the social circle I'd fallen into by rote, transposing mainstream to gaystream as if being palatable and assimilative would've kept me as close to normal as possible, close enough to follow the golden path my parents had laid out for me. I liked massages, high-end resorts, and sesame-encrusted ahi tuna, but not at the cost. I wouldn't have begrudged my parents their luxuries and their golf, the hard-earned rewards that were unimaginable to them as kids, if, somewhere in this class upgrade, they'd kept a space for me to comfortably express myself. But they hadn't, so I picked on the one trait that tied my parents to my brother's friends. "Oh, you mean wealthy."

"Rich? You don't know anything about it! What, you think we're rich?" My mom turned into a wounded bear, clawing back at the attacker she'd just treated to three very expensive days. "You're the one that's rich," she shouted. Following a Merlot-inspired logic, she spat out numbers, using my hourly rate to estimate my salary, shocked as she did the math. "You're rich," she said. "You're the one that's rich."

She had the gist of my earnings, even though her calculations were slightly off, failing to account for my four-day work week, my own negotiation based on my preference for time over money, and my regular school loan payments. I lived more cheaply than she could've imagined, and had been hoarding my money since landing the travel dot-com gig. I had more than enough to go on a trip, not a short two-week vacation like Scotland, but a backpacking adventure in Asia, Central America, or Africa. That's what I'd always done—saved, picked a budget travel location, and disappeared for months on end. But this time my "travel fund" was earmarked for the journey I wasn't ready to make, the one that would separate me completely from *people like us,* who didn't have top surgery, even though we were the only ones who could afford it.

"Can somebody please help me," my dad begged. We were at the same closed on-ramp again.

My mom jabbed her finger at the GPS keypad, finding another route. I stared out the window in silence, until we were on the highway. The wind circulated through the crack in the window. "What, you're not talking to me now?" my mom said. "You're mad at me?"

"I'm not mad." I tilted my head against the glass. "I'm just sad."

On day seven, the final night, at my request we ate dinner at a gourmet vegetarian restaurant. In the theater district, at the bottom of a hotel, the place had a gloomy, fine-dining-for-business-travelers atmosphere. Even though neither of my parents were hardcore carnivores, watching them hold their menus for so long concerned me.

"Are you going to be okay?" I asked my dad. His cheeks were sunburned, his eyes glazed with exhaustion. He'd had a long afternoon chasing my mom around the city, and he nodded amenably, closing his menu as the waiter arrived.

"So, let me get this straight," my dad said to the waiter. "There

are no hidden hamburgers? No code word for chicken?" His charm
trickled out, lacking its usual vigor. He mustered a weak smile before ordering hand-cut frites.

"You ordered french fries!" my mom yelled, chastising him
with a few shakes of her head. She then proceeded to ask the
waiter about every ingredient on the menu. "What's vegan sour
cream?" she asked.

"It's a white nut-based sauce, sour in flavor."

"Veggie sausage?"

"Spicy seitan. It's wheat gluten."

"Tempeh?"

"Soy based. A cousin of tofu."

For me, reading the menu was like scanning the crowd at a
queer bar—the possibilities endlessly enticing. But listening to my
mom try to translate this new food language into something she
understood, watching my father too tired to try and order french
fries, made me regret bringing them to this restaurant. Whether
they enjoyed their food or not, they vacuumed up all three of their
courses, licking the last pools of sauce off the empty plates with
their forks.

"Are you glad we're leaving?" my mom asked once my dad ex-
cused himself to the bathroom. I shook my head, refusing to take
her bait. "Well, we love it out here," she continued. "This was so
fun, honey. Maybe next time we'll go to Sonoma."

It had been a great visit, I thought to myself—seven days with
my parents and only one real fight. I'd tried harder than usual to
avoid confrontation, as if I knew it would be our last time together
and I wanted to preserve the memory.

"It's hard when your kids live so far away." My mom lifted
her glasses to wipe away a tear, reminding me of visiting days at
sleepaway camp when I'd break into hysterics, begging her not to
leave me. "I know, Mom, I know." She wrapped her muscular pipe
cleaner of an arm around me and pulled me close, recoiling when
my dad returned.

Under the table, my dad handed me "the wad"—the name my

brother and I had come up with for a chunk of cash so thick we could never tell how many twenties were in there until we counted later. My dad had been handing us the good-bye wad for as long as we could remember. Usually he'd say, "I hope this helps a little," and it always did, even now that I supported myself. I told my dad I was finally going to get a winter jacket, something I'd been too frugal to buy myself, with his gift. Through his fatigue, he broke into his benevolent smile, the one I strived to emulate.

At the front door, I hugged them both again. Before leaving, my dad placed his hand on my shoulder. His parting words came out gently. "I hope this is just a phase," he said, holding my gaze with his tender, tired eyes. "I want my little girl back."

Eleven

THE NEW WORLD

Before I could catch my breath from my parents' visit, or process my dad's last words, he sent me a follow-up e-mail. Reading it in my cubicle at work, I felt like we were still standing in the dismal entrance of that restaurant-hotel, my dad not yet finished with his closing remarks. My mom must have told him what I'd said in the hot tub because he was basically begging me not to do something drastic or catastrophic. Knowing my father, I had to assume he meant an operation, a possibility now so real to him, he'd gone into panic mode.

In his letter, his vision of me, shared with the great pride of a father, made me feel ill, the word *woman* alone turning my breakfast cereal to a carb lump in my stomach. Despite his anguished, affectionate tone, certain phrases, synonymous with the ones raged upon me as a kid, hit the spot that had never healed, linking my fury and pain in the tears dripping from my eyes. His belief that I was throwing away my chance of happiness was the antithesis of how I experienced my own evolution.

The sporty girl with the long ponytail and small hoop earrings had faded many years ago, and now, confronted with my frantic father trying to bring her back, I was certain there was nothing left to our wasted relationship but his torment, my guilt, and a fight over ownership of my body, image, and identity. I reread his e-mail over and over in a state of catatonic sorrow until I finally noticed my wet keyboard, the fluorescent lights, coworkers all around me, and I fled the office.

Later that night, when I'd calmed down some, I printed out his e-mail and read it repeatedly, as if trying to take into my bones what I knew to be true in my head. The "operation" incident, his good-bye plea, this letter making a case for his image of me—the barrage of his fatherhood with all its beloved intent would be relentless if I replied, a pickax gradually chipping away at me.

I folded his letter and placed it in my wallet, next to the cash for the jacket I couldn't bring myself to buy with money I didn't need or ask for, and decided not to engage, finally setting a boundary. I understood fully that by ignoring him, I was restricting his role, setting myself up to break our contract. I would no longer permit him to express his feelings about me, to oversee everything I did, thereby giving up all the future wads and relinquishing the safety net. But as much as I wanted to toss off the golden handcuffs right then, they represented the last vestige of connection to my dad, and that was a lot harder to give up.

Distancing myself by disregarding my dad had an instantaneous and extraordinary effect. My flat-chested fantasy, the elevator music that had been in the background for nearly two years, immediately developed a steady thumping bass line. Like a heartbeat, it was with me when I ran, practiced yoga, took a shower, put on my binder, ate cereal, rode the bus; my daydream was so continuous, my thoughts so repetitive that I had a hard time keeping track of when I spoke them, when I was silent, and how much time passed between each time I said, "Is it worth the money? How unattractive are the scars? Will it hurt?"

I shared these concerns with Derek, a combined extrovert/introvert type like me who could socialize and party all night, then spend the next week reading novels, working out, and claiming "alone time," which was really just "home time" because he and I were spending so much of ours together that we'd quickly become best friends. He filled a void I hadn't noticed until he'd arrived, that of a very close friendship with a male roommate. He was also my first gay one, and we shared a homoerotic intimacy that was both playful and meaningful—he objectified me in a man-on-man way that made me feel truly seen. When I rambled about my chest, he patiently listened, acting as a sounding board so I could hear myself—I heard that my considerations had moved from the theoretical to practical realm, and that I wanted comfort in my body, independent of gender.

Although I considered bringing up the subject of surgery with Greg before a yoga class, and Bec once when he was over for dinner, I was afraid of being influenced in any way by something they could say. I also kept quiet around Jess, not wanting to be impacted by his intellect, persuasive oratory, or the issues he was working out for himself. If I were to talk with Jess, I would need to employ reason and arm myself with brainpower, the very things that I sought to silence upon experiencing the briefest and most fleeting moments, often in my yoga classes, of peace from my mind. Underneath and in between the distractions in my head emerged that which defied logic and control, actual feelings—the one thing Jess and I had never talked about with any vulnerability and honesty.

He must've been keeping to himself as well, because he waited until after he'd made a consultation appointment with Dr. Brownstein to tell me. I shouldn't have been too surprised, since Melissa had mentioned his intent eight months earlier, but so much time had passed, I hadn't really believed he'd go through with it. I still didn't, until, a week later, we were headed to a new evening yoga class together. Walking down the subtle hill of our quiet residential area to the pattering rhythm of his flip-flops, he made his announcement. "I'm having top surgery," he said. "I set a date and everything." His date was mid-November, about a month away.

"Oh my god. Wow," I said. "Congratulations."

His smile spread slowly, curving up from the center of his lips. I searched for uncertainty or his trademark confident overcompensation, but he looked content, no doubt or second-guesses hidden in the recesses. "I can't wait," he said.

"That's really amazing," I said. "I'm so happy for you."

And I was, not just happy, but proud of him. He must have reconciled his career fears, his hospital trauma, accepted that he could make this change without becoming a man. Stopping at the corner, I noticed the mat rolled under his arm, the early dusk of autumn falling, the studio that would grow dark during class with only the flickers of candles for light. I wondered how much he'd settled in there, if maybe we'd been sharing in each other's process without talking, but with our mats side by side, listening for our own voices, finding our self-trust, learning to love our bodies in all of their imperfect perfection. That's where I was slowly leaving behind my own fears and concerns, where I was often dedicating my practice to my dad, holding him in my heart even as I solidified in my bones the decision to cut him out of my life.

As we approached the studio, I asked Jess his impressions of Brownstein, if the renowned doctor, notorious for his lack of bed-side manner, was as coarse as everyone claimed. Jess validated his matter-of-fact attitude, but chalked it up to surgeon's demeanor. "I really liked him," he said.

I pictured Jess roaming around the house with a towel wrapped around his waist, ironing his T-shirts while topless, brushing his teeth in his boxer briefs, the daily sight of him advertising exactly what I wanted. And I knew at that moment, for sure, that I would go through with it myself. "I'm about a year away," I told him.

"Take your time," he said, as he opened the studio door.

A year had been a completely arbitrary amount of time, and right after I said it, I knew it was only the safety of far far away that had allowed me to verbalize my certainty. But once I stated my intention, it took on the power of a driving force.

Ever since my parents' visit, I'd been making excuses to avoid my weekly lunchtime phone call to my mother. Initially, I hadn't wanted to end up in a discussion about my dad and his e-mail. It's not that she would've defended him, but she would've done anything to keep our family together, and since she had no sway or impact on him, the onus fell on me. It would've been hard to talk to her about top surgery; it would've been even harder to tell her that my dad and I had reached our last stand and my seat at the dinner table would soon remain empty, we would no longer be a family. I was building up to both, so consumed with thoughts about surgery that I couldn't even feign a discussion about anything else. A few days after my conversation with Jess, I sent my mother a brief e-mail to tell her I was "going through some stuff" and would let her know when I was ready to talk.

Then I returned to the website Bec had told me about checking out long ago—the repository of headless before-and-after top-surgery photos. I began clicking through big breasts and small breasts, long straight scars and short cupped scars, fat bodies and thin bodies. In about half of the pictures, hair and muscles camouflaged the healing chests—a bonus of testosterone, which preceded top surgery for many people. Trying to envision my surgery results, I ignored the guys on testosterone, a hormone I wasn't considering. Facial hair, a deep voice, being recognized or identifying as a man had never been connected to my desire for a flat chest—something that I'd stopped associating exclusively with men, even though that was the easiest way to describe my self-image to someone like my mother. But Bec had a flat chest, Jess would have one, and the possibilities for design-your-own gender-malleable identities, creative neither/nor gender expressions, were growing every day in my queer subculture; they would have greater currency when more people could see and understand them.

The pictures showed chests swollen and bruised, incisions raw and red. The lines were symmetrical, at least in Brownstein's work, which I deemed the best, but they were still huge gashes sewn shut with hundreds of stitches. I reminded myself that I despised anything medical, fainted at the sight of my own blood, and grew queasy if I heard *hematoma* instead of *bruise*. I clicked and clicked, and in the very best images, those chests captured a year out, the imperfections still glared at me until all I could see were deflated balloons marred by scars. I thought of Bec's chest, not quite perfect, yet pretty damn close, the flat white lines melding into his ivory skin. He'd arrived at this end not caring what his chest would look like. As he'd once said, "Anything was better than having breasts." I checked out well over a hundred pictures trying to decide if this held true for me.

Eventually, I clicked over to Brownstein's site and the linked blogs and testimonials. On one page, there was a sideways shot of a man holding a surfboard in the shallow ocean, a wetsuit rolled to his waist, and in huge block letters, it read, "Thank you for making this a reality." On another page, a buff guy posed with his arms aloft, flexing his biceps, the beam of his smile, his effervescent pride, a distraction from his chest scars. I followed links through to YouTube videos, landing on one of an attractive guy with a goatee who'd been on testosterone for two years while saving the $8,000 for top surgery. He made his confessional-style video the night before, and at the very end, he grabbed two handfuls of flesh through his T-shirt. "Finally," he said, and broke into a heaving sob, the explosion of his relief reverberating through me as if it were my own. He wiped his face with the back of his hand, making a swift recovery, but I did not, the tears still streaming down my face.

Alone in my room, surrounded by my bare beige walls, my mind started to spin around the images of disfigurement and stigmatization, the inescapable depth of desire I shared with the people in these blogs, testimonials, and videos. I folded down the screen on my laptop. My sole decoration, a world map tacked above my fireplace, stared back at me, revealing only the futility of flight, the breasts that would come with me to India, Nepal, or South Africa. I felt dread block my throat. Wind whooshed through the chimney, barreling down the hill outside; a jog was out of the question. I opened the weed drawer and was overcome with the rare instinct to close it. I caught the time on my travel alarm clock.

It was a quarter till the next yoga class. I'd memorized the schedule for the same reason alcoholics memorized AA meetings, for emergencies—mine was needing a minute-by-minute reminder to breathe.

I was inside the studio with time to spare. On my mat, I lay down on my back and stretched my arms and legs into a long straight line. Staring up at the ceiling, I envisioned my breasts crumbling away like an old stone statue, my empty sports bra falling off to the side. This could be so easy, I told myself, just get rid of them—three hours under anesthesia plus two weeks off work and I'd be free forever. I would call Brownstein, make a consultation. I had the money, I could do this. There was no reason I couldn't do this.

The teacher, an elfish Jewish guy who chanted like the cantor from my bat mitzvah, soon began our movements with cat and cow flows. On my hands and knees, I dropped my stomach, arched my back, and practiced letting go of self-consciousness with a deep "Moo." I lifted my stomach to my spine, rounded my back and shoulders, and in the middle of my scaredy-cat "Rrrwww," I felt a sucker punch to my gut as I suddenly thought of the scar on my shoulder.

I couldn't believe I'd looked through hundreds of pictures online without thinking about the keloid scar on my upper right arm. It had resulted from a mosquito bite I overscratched when I was eleven, and for the rest of my adolescence I treated this hard, raised bump, about the size of a button on a woman's dress shirt, as if it were the worst flaw imaginable, single-handedly destroying all of my potential to be beautiful.

People around me raised legs, wrapped arms, and although I tried to follow along, I kept returning to memories of trying to hide my scar, the head tilt I maintained to drape my hair across it at the beach, the T-shirt I wore under my varsity basketball team tank top, and finally the skin-colored Band-Aid I taped across it for every game during a traveling softball season with awful sleeveless polyester uniforms. It was after the summer of the Band-Aid tan line, as if that was less glaring than a small scar, that I went to a dermatologist and received a cortisone shot that broke up the tissue.

As I placed my hands together as if in prayer and twisted in a lunge, I barely noticed the flat white spot on my shoulder. But the distress, as well as my susceptibility to keloids, was still with me. I got into child's pose and took a mental inventory of my body, the formerly pierced earlobe that had a hard lump, the scar near my left armpit that did not. The debate with myself over whether top surgery was worth the risk of excessive scarring continued un-abated. I was relieved when frog pose was called, knowing the end of class was near.

I folded my mat to pad my knees, splayed my legs like a frog, and leaned forward onto my elbows in a position meant to be held for a while. The teacher began to tell a story, and with nowhere to go, stuck with my legs about to snap out of their sockets, I tuned in. He spoke of a forest full of big strong trees, their branches flush with foliage, and of a storm. Lightning struck one of the trees, splicing it, severing the trunk into raw splinters of wood.

I felt the hands of an assistant on my shoulders, the physical "hello" before an adjustment that came only once or twice a class, the release I jonesed for. The hands moved to my waist, slowly pulling my hips back as my pelvis dropped to the floor. I expected the hands to stop. I always expected the hands to stop, thinking that my body couldn't possibly go any farther.

The teacher spoke of the unpreventable, undeniable force that was this lightning, before returning to the gashed, mangled tree. "It's still beautiful," the teacher said in a sweet, angelic tone. "So, so beautiful," he repeated as the helping hands guided my body into a space I could not find on my own. I took a deep, nourishing breath, imagined the beauty of that scarred tree, and exhaled my adolescent trauma.

Yoga had become many things to me, but whenever I tried to hone in on a specific effect it belittled the profound power this

practice had upon my life. It was whatever it offered that day, whatever I opened to, and on this day, it was a parable, the support of a
stranger, the time to let go of the last thing blocking my way.

For the next week, I intended to call Dr. Brownstein for a consultation appointment, finally mentioning it to Ramona, with whom
I was now having regular instant message conversations during
the workday. After barely talking for five months, I hoped we were
both ready to be friends and had convinced myself that confid-
ing in my ex and instigating immediate closeness was like playing
with bang snaps rather than dynamite. "I usually tell someone I'm
about to do something when I want to be held accountable," Ramona wrote in an instant message.

"That's probably why I'm telling you," I replied.

"Call Brownstein. You're ready."

I considered asking Ramona or another friend to go with me
to my consultation, but instinct told me I needed to go by myself.
It's how I'd know I could stand alone behind a decision that was
exclusively for me. For the two weeks leading up to the appointment, all I could think about was logistics and whether it would be
possible to have surgery before the Christmas holiday so I could
still catch some of the snowboarding season, thoughts that proved
to me I was, in fact, ready.

On the morning of my consultation, I filled an entire sheet
of yellow legal paper with questions while scanning the online
before-and-after pictures again. With my paper in my back pocket,
I rode my bike the two miles to the live/work space, excited to meet
the man behind the legend. Performing top surgeries for nearly
thirty years, Brownstein was one of the few surgeons who didn't
hide his specialty underneath pamphlets for breast reductions.

Brownstein's dachshund Frank greeted me at the door of what
seemed more like a home business or a small dot-com than a doctor's office. The place was tastefully decorated with textiles and art,

including a metal sculpture, a sort of Tin Man Tit Man with long pointy rocket breasts standing in the corner like a sentinel.

As I walked farther into the office, I caught a woman behind a computer singing to herself, "The Nina, the Pinta, the Santa Maria." When she looked up, she noticed me. "Oh my, I'm so sorry," she said. "I'm so so sorry."

The assistant was blond and reminded me of some kind of "ist," a cosmetologist or a dental hygienist. I was curious if it was her general lack of professionalism that distressed her, or if she knew that calling attention to a feminine name, potentially a source of pain for someone seeking gender reassignment surgery, wasn't the smoothest move. "It's totally okay," I said.

"I'm just so embarrassed."

"Really, it's okay. People have been saying that to me my whole life." As I spoke, suddenly aware that that may have been the final time I'd inspire that memorable string of ships, an unexpected sadness overwhelmed me.

Now that I no longer felt constrained by how my decisions would impact my parents, I'd begun to consider changing my name. Although I'd revisited every gender-neutral or masculine N name in the baby book, I had allegiance to "Nick" for popping up at a time when the boy in me was begging to be seen, if only by me, in my own mind. Lately, I'd been considering "Nic" versus "Nick," but my preference for the latter was more of a creative than a gendered interest. I liked the way my first and last names linked together with the double K. Thinking about a new name had been fun, except I hadn't fully realized that to take one on, I'd have to give up the word that had been closest to me for thirty years.

When the "ist" stopped apologizing, she sat on the other side of a solid wood desk and explained much of what I already knew about the surgery center, the five payment installments, and the series of follow-up appointments. She reminded me of a favorite aunt, an adult who didn't understand kid things but whom you talked to instead of your mom. "Will you be transgendering?" she asked.

I imagined this was her synonym for transition, but did she want to know if I'd be changing my name, switching to an *M* on my driver's license, taking testosterone, considering bottom surgery, if I used the men's or women's bathroom, or which dressing room I was sent into at a department store? "I'm not sure I know what you mean," I said.

"Oh, oh," she said in that desperately apologetic tone of hers. "You don't have to get into it. I just need to note whether to refer to you as 'he' or 'she' at the center."

I wanted to calm this flustered woman, tell her she was doing a fine job and I felt safe and comfortable in the office. I also wanted to tell her that a simple pronoun query would suffice and perhaps we could retire the term *transgendering* along with *sex-change operation*. Instead, I told her "she" was fine.

She asked if I had any questions, and I did, a whole sheet of them, all of which would have to wait for the doc. She pulled out a large appointment book and offered me a few dates in the middle and end of January. I asked if she had anything earlier. She flipped some pages, talking about how busy it was around the Christmas holidays with school breaks. "I could probably get you in on December third," she said. "Would you like that?"

My stomach dropped out. That was less than six weeks away.

"I'll have to check with Dr. Brownstein to see if he can squeeze you in." She barely glanced up from the book.

As I waited to see if my nervousness would expand into reality-induced fear, an all-consuming excitement took over. "That would be great."

The assistant walked up to the loft and asked Brownstein, returning to say it was no problem, he would do two surgeries on the third.

"Should I be concerned about being 'squeezed in' for what I consider major surgery?" I asked.

"Not at all," she said. "He's the best."

"Any chance I could get the first appointment that day?" I was only half kidding.

Brownstein's shoes clanked as he came down the metal stairs. Tall and wiry with a full head of distinguished white hair, he had smooth skin that made him appear younger than I'd expected. "This is what I tell people," he said. "If they're the first one of the day, I say I'm fresh, and if they're the second one, I tell them I'm all warmed up."

I laughed. "So, it's no problem?" I asked, aware that what might've felt like putting him out was the equivalent of offering him five grand to work a few hours of overtime. "How many do you do in a day?"

"Three was the most," he said. "It was a rare circumstance. Everything went fine. No problems. But I won't do it again."

Brownstein told me he did four to six surgeries a week. I asked if he took enough vacation and whether he'd have a nice rest over Thanksgiving, since it was the week before my scheduled date.

He assured me he rested and replaced his assistant behind the desk. He walked me through the surgical logistics, everything I'd heard or read, including his inability to guarantee results and that the extent of scarring, the likelihood of keloids, was mostly determined by genes.

I unfolded my yellow sheet of legal paper. "Sometimes when I see guys running with their shirts off, their pecs bounce. Will my pecs bounce?"

"Depends on your pecs," he said.

"I figure with mammary tissue removed, I won't have 'breast soreness,' but will I have PMS symptoms in my chest?"

"I can't imagine how you could," he said, sounding slightly baffled. "It's also not the kind of thing my patients would mention."

"Will losing more weight help my results?"

"No."

"What if I have the surgery and then I gain a whole lot of weight, what will happen?" I thought my chest might explode.

"It probably won't look so good."

I figured he'd tell me to cool it with the absurd questions, but when I prompted him to shut me up, he only said, "I've got time. I don't have any appointments for a while."

I moved to nipple grafts, drains, how much assistance I'd need during my recovery ("very little"), and ended with the fine print on the medical waiver. "So about the blood clotting and this thrombosis," I said. "What's the risk of me dying here?"

Brownstein stared at me solemnly, and I saw in his eyes that he never forgot the seriousness of what he did, bearing responsibility in the operating room while his patients slept peacefully. He reiterated his smooth track record, which covered a few decades and over a thousand surgeries. "There are always risks," he said. "I don't think we need to talk about them. You're going to be just fine." He knocked on the wood desk. I trusted him completely.

He looked over my form once more and focused on the question I had evaded about the "therapist's letter." I knew from friends and blogs that he, chairman of the Ethics Committee for the World Professional Association for Transgender Health, didn't always require this letter, recommended in the association's guidelines for gender reassignment surgery.

"Do I have to?" I asked.

"Can you?"

"I *can*," I said. "I'd prefer not to." I was paying $8,000 out of my own pocket. Health insurance wouldn't cover surgery. Why did I need a damn permission slip? I fought my urge to argue. I didn't want to piss off one of the few surgeons who could do this type of procedure. "What does it have to say?" I asked. "I'm of sound mind to make an adult decision?"

"That's it, nothing more." He assured me the letter would sit in some dusty file in the bottom of some dusty drawer.

"Fine." I aimed for a placating tone.

We went around the divider to the only part of his office with anything sterile or medical. Brownstein sat in a plastic chair far from the exam table. He crossed his legs effeminately and waited.

I pulled my shirt over my head, then my binder. I stood in the center of the room.

"Yep, I can do it," he said, remaining a few feet away.

I asked him a question about the incisions and one of my birthmarks. He came closer and pointed to a few places on my chest, treating my breasts as I did, flesh to be excised. Relieved, I had my shirt back on in less than five minutes.

Brownstein left his assistant to make my follow-up appointments. She was still shaken by the Christopher Columbus situation. "It's such a pretty name," she said. "Nina."

Her last word echoed in my heart. I lingered on the sounds, traced the curves, had breakup sex with my name right there in the office, holding on as we moved in opposite directions.

"And it's quite popular these days," she said.

Growing up, I didn't meet more than one or two people with my name. Now, I tried to imagine elementary schools full of these small Ninas. I pictured them with long wavy hair pulled back into barrettes, pierced ears with rhinestone studs, beige corduroy pants with the cuffs rolled up. I pictured them as I was once, a little girl snuggled into a red peacoat, her father bending down to button it and squeezing her too tightly.

Shortly after my father sent me the e-mail I still carried in my wallet, he'd sent me a follow-up, stating that the first might have confused me and to please call him. When I called almost two months later, he was relieved to hear from me. He shut the door to his office and asked about the weather and other banalities before shifting to his e-mail clarification.

It was my lunch break on a sunny Wednesday. I sat on the edge of a stone fountain in the financial district, surrounded by pods of people in business-casual dress eating salads and sandwiches. Holding my cell phone to my ear, I listened to him reiterate that I was not seeing myself for the young woman I was, I was throwing away my chance at happiness, and he was afraid I would do something extreme.

Our break had done nothing to calm him. He was a soda can,

dropped, shaken, and placed back on the shelf, waiting for me to pop the top. You'd think I'd stolen government-subsidized lunch money from school kids or ripped off an elderly Meals On Wheels program from the horror with which he spoke about gender variance, the monstrosity of simply being different.

I pleaded with him to stop, telling him that if he continued, I wouldn't be able to talk to him anymore. Only upon hearing my own desperation did I realize I'd been hoping for an apology, the one thing that would prevent me from doing what I'd planned. But he perceived my begging as a threat, and we fell into the worn grooves of our arguments, the same tired fight where he tried to use the power of fatherhood to control me, and I shut down, trying to hold tough, except now I was too old to sing the "Somewhere over the rainbow" refrain in my head until he was done forcing his opinion, stance, argument, and rhetoric, disguised as questions, down on me.

I turned away from the lunchtime crowd and walked toward the Bay, searching the choppy gray water for courage. Underneath the bridge, an enormous freighter chugged along, headed out to the open sea. "It's unhealthy for me to be in a relationship with you right now," I said. "I can't talk to you for a while."

"That's it? You're cutting off contact with your father? You can't do that," he said. "I'm your dad. What, I'm not allowed to ask you questions?"

His questions were, "First you were normal, then gay, now this—what happened?" and, "Where are you getting information? Are you talking to the right people?" I let him berate me with these questions because I was partially convinced he was entitled, but mostly because I didn't want to say good-bye when there was no hello in sight. I thought of everything I could lose, my generous father who'd taken me to a Guns N' Roses and Metallica concert in middle school, my patient father who'd talked me through my bedbug scare of '07, my sensitive father who might be too offended after this call to ever talk to me again, my aging father who could have a heart attack any day. I forced the fatal thoughts from my head, told myself we'd be different people when we met again, capable of having an honest, healthy relationship.

"You're not thinking of becoming transgender, are you?" he asked.

"I am transgender," I snapped, surprising myself with my own clear pronouncement.

He'd probably researched the term, considered himself educated on the subject by reading articles in the *New York Times* and watching episodes of *Dateline, 20/20,* and *60 Minutes* with slow-motion animation of the *Diagnostic and Statistical Manual* opening to Gender Identity Disorder and encapsulated by the headline "Born in the Wrong Body"—none of which spoke to me and my experience. I am transgender, I thought, I *am* transgender.

"Are you considering doing something about this?" my dad asked.

"I don't know," I lied.

In almost every way, my father had been a perfect parent. His one failing was minor, microscopic, and yet it was as strong as a tab of acid. He had never been able to support that which he didn't condone. "I need your support," I said. "I'll only accept one hundred percent support."

"You need my support, you don't support me. You question the way I live my life."

I tried to picture him in his office, overdressed for the casual environment, legal-size manila folders and a picture of our family on his desk, but all I could see was a scared man, his knees pressed into his chest in a dark, lonely room, pushing away his child.

"I will only take complete support from you," I repeated.

"You think people are supporting you now, but they won't be there forever." He jutted off on a tangent about his mother's multiple sclerosis and how all of her friends stopped showing up, slowly abandoning her as she crawled toward death. My empathy for his mother and for him, a child forced into the role of caretaker too early, only encouraged his digression.

Finally, I told him that I wasn't sick and that I trusted my friends to stick by me, but his doubt and fear had crept into me. What if something went wrong with the anesthesia during surgery or an unexpected complication occurred—would my friends still be there for me?

"If you're so worried about people leaving me, then you be there for me," I said. For as different as issues of gender and sexuality were, I couldn't help but meld them, playing catch-up on our unresolved history, the hurt I still carried from his persistent denial and silence, his embarrassment and disappointment about who I was. "I've been gay for ten years," I said. "Tell me, what have you done to support me?"

I could hear his appalled inhalation from three thousand miles away. "I don't vote against gay rights. I vote for gay marriage."

I considered thanking him for not voting me into a cage, proving that I was equally incapable of holding up my end of a rational, nonconfrontational conversation. "I love you very much," I said. "But I can't talk to you for a while. Please don't call me. Please don't e-mail me."

"You don't love me," he said. "If you loved me . . ."

"I love you," I said.

"No, you don't—"

I cut him off. Like a small child who covers his ears while shouting "La La La La La," I blocked my dad out, repeating, "I love you . . . I love you . . . I love you. . . ." and hung up the phone.

Twelve

MAMA'S BOYS

With one month to my big day, I turned all my attention to preparation. I locked down my two most outwardly loving, affectionate, touchy-feeling friends to escort me to my surgery and secured
promises of recovery help from others. A few days after cutting off
contact with my dad, I wrote my mom a long e-mail, believing we
now had the space to at least attempt communication without my
dad storming in and taking over. I also considered it too cruel to
undergo a procedure with some risk and not inform my mom (and
my dad by extension); they were parents, above all, their concern
for my physical health unquestionable.

Although I joked grimly to my friends that you're not really
trans until you lose a parent, my attempt at humor fell short at the
idea of losing two. The e-mail I sent my mother was guarded and
almost completely informational, the entire tone very matter of
fact; the subject line might as well have read: FYI . . . I'm having
top surgery.

In my letter, I shared my discomfort with my breasts, cring-
ing as I typed those last two words, and that I understood myself
best through the term *transgender*, which I defined as anyone who
doesn't fit into the traditional categories of man or woman. For
context, I offered some of the options available to trans people—
name changes, pronoun changes, and hormones—but in my case,
I focused entirely on my top-surgery decision. In several paragraphs I provided digestible information about the procedure, as

well as my confidence in Brownstein (with a link to his website) to calm her practical fears.

Only at the end did I exhibit anything that could be associated with emotions, and I kept my distance from them, even as I wrote of my own struggle, acknowledging for the first time that a couple years ago, underneath my eagerness to learn from The Boys, there was a depth of alarm, fear that if I was really like them, I was better off dead. My fright had arrived most often in the middle of the night, when my guard was down, and I'd always pushed it away by morning in order to get through the next day. Even in a letter, I hated to place that period of hardship anywhere near my surgery decision, which was made from a place of stability and joy, grounded in love for the body I wanted to inhabit. But I hoped to empathize with my mom, let her know that it had taken me time to accept my new path, and I understood it would take her time, as well. I left her with book, blog, and group resources, and as nicely as I could, I told her I was too focused on myself to carry her right now. Offering her little, I asked for little in return, requesting only that she tell me she supported and loved me.

"Really, it's pretty simple," I typed in an instant message to my brother after I sent the letter to my mom and him. "The people who can be there for me one hundred percent are invited to be in my life. Those who can't, aren't."

"Should I expect an Evite?" he replied.

I busted out laughing at my desk, hearing the humor behind the voice I missed. At the start of the fall, he'd moved to England to work at a boarding school, and with an eight-hour time difference, gone were the daily calls we'd both depended on to survive our breakups. His had happened shortly before mine, and in the wake of his devastation, he'd moved abroad, stating his inspiration came from my solo travels. Our regular postbreakup talks had brought us into a period of extreme closeness for a few months, much like our time living together in Jackson Hole, our backpacking trips abroad, our entire childhood. One difficult conversation in New Hampshire the year before could not make a long-term dent in a

NINA HERE NOR THERE   *183*

brother-sister relationship that had begun so long ago I couldn't even remember our earliest times together.

He typed to me that he was in a different place, figuratively and literally, from that challenging conversation. My experience of gender was still foreign to him, but his breakup had aged him, forced him to fend for himself, taught him that he alone was responsible for creating his own happiness, something that as I'd tossed him bits and pieces of information leading up to my decision, he encouraged me to create for myself. I too was in a different place than I had been during that earlier conversation, now confident about something I had only been exploring then. And my brother, a straight white guy, hadn't been the best person to work out my gender self-questioning with, but as had been the case our whole lives, once I told him where I was going, he'd come along for the ride, even if he couldn't find our destination on the map.

He volunteered to call our mother later, to make sure she was okay after receiving my letter, a helping hand I appreciated and hadn't anticipated. With a continent and ocean between us, he seemed so very far away, and I'd prepared myself to expect nothing from him, or anyone in my family. Having made sure I could go through this procedure alone, with the assistance of friends, my only hope for my mom was that she not hurt me with her response. But it was hard to deny how envious I felt thinking about Sylvia, Jess's mom, who was about to arrive to take care of him.

I anxiously counted down the last few days to Jess's surgery, aware that I would have to go through the recovery twice, first as observer to my own fate, then as participant. On the morning of his big day, I made sure I was up early enough to wish him well. Distracted and preoccupied, he nodded with minimal acknowledgment before sticking his keys and phone in his pocket. "Can I give you a hug?" I asked. After three years of living with our rooms side by side, our gender and yoga journeys intertwined, he was, in many ways, the person closest to me, and yet that was our first embrace.

It may have been the only time we'd ever touched one another. "Good luck, brother," I whispered as he disappeared down the backstairs with his mother.

A few hours later, I received the text informing me that his surgery had gone well, and that's when I got really nervous. Fearful of finding Jess on the couch in agony, I made my way home slowly that evening. I was pleasantly surprised to open the door to a celebration, our living room full of friends, and a coherent, content Jess propped up in the armchair. An oversized button-down shirt draped his thick, padded chest, the mark of a purple pen still visible on his neck.

As his mother recounted the simple drive to the center, the valet parking, the kind staff, and the quick in-and-out surgery that had them home by midday, she referred to Jess as "she" and "Jessica." The rest of us used male pronouns for him. Although everybody in the room must have noticed, nobody seemed to care. Sylvia put our whole house at ease, bestowing upon us all "dears," "sweethearts," and other tokens of affection in a voice as comforting as the homemade chicken noodle soup simmering on the stove. Listening to her describe the day's events relieved much of my own anxiety, and by the time all of our guests left, my only lingering concern surrounded the notorious drains. I'd been assured by Brownstein that I could empty the fluid from these contraptions twice a day alone, but I was worried about my squeamishness and propensity to faint. Timidly, I asked Jess and his mom if I could watch this part. "Come on, sweetie," Sylvia said, her white nightgown trailing as she led me into Jess's room.

I summoned my composure and steeled myself for the grossout factor as Jess, seated in a chair from our kitchen, unbuttoned his shirt. Clipped to the bottom of his elastic bandage, on either side of his belly button, two grenade-shaped receptacles held small amounts of red liquid. Unable to see where the tubes, covered by all the padding, entered his body, I tricked myself into seeing the setup as a couple of water balloons with colored dye hanging on hollow plastic strings.

Sylvia knelt before him and undid the safety pin that tethered one of the balloons to his wrap. "You want to massage out any clots," she said, gripping the tube with the thumb and first two fingers of one hand. Using the same fingers on the other hand, she squeezed then slid along the tube as if playing a musical instrument.

"Do you have to worry about the pressure?" I asked. "Will the receptacle explode when you open it?"

"It shouldn't," she replied. "I'm going to cover it with a towel, just in case." She held the receptacle in one hand, rested the towel over it, and used her other hand to flip the plastic stopper open. Jess sat there silent and vulnerable as I'd ever seen him, letting his mom lead the caretaking dance.

Sylvia poured the contents into a measuring cup and Jess recorded the time and exact amount, somewhere in the two-tablespoon range, on a piece of paper. Sylvia pressed the air out of the receptacle before closing the stopper and reattaching the clip to his bandage. I watched silently as she did the other one. "Easy," she said.

"I can do that," I replied, energized by my relief. "I can definitely do that by myself." I smiled at Jess, who looked happy but exhausted, and said good night to them both.

Lying in bed, I could hardly believe how much just seeing Jess in his peaceful, somewhat drugged state, had alleviated my anxiety. I was certain that I had all the support and resources I needed for my turn in three weeks, but listening to Sylvia flit around in the guest room behind me made me yearn for the one thing I still wanted: my mommy.

My mom's response to my e-mail had arrived a few days before, less than twenty-four hours after I had sent it, and she'd offered the two things I'd explicitly requested. She'd also included a few sentences of apology and support from my dad. I passed along my appreciation for his note through my mom, but made sure she knew I was not open to any direct contact with him. I simply did not trust him; he'd spilled his emotions onto me too many times, burdened me too much with his pain, consistently doubted and questioned me to a debilitating degree. Excluding him was selfish, but damn did it feel good to make a positive move for myself that he couldn't taint.

There is a reason flight attendants instruct you to put on your oxygen mask first before helping others; once I had placed my own needs first, I surprised myself by how much I was able to be there for my mother as she struggled with my news. Her ignorant questions and sadness no longer threatened me. I was secure enough to reiterate and explain myself over and over with total calm. She surprised me, too, with her composure, and although I wondered if shutting out my dad had served as a warning of what could happen, as we continued to speak, I could feel her loneliness, how little she had in this world, and that she didn't need an example— she wasn't going to give up her kid for anything. I finally felt safe.

In these conversations, long and carefully controlled like our tennis matches had once been, I shared with her every detail of Jess's swift recovery, dropping "Jess's mom" this and "Jess's mom" that as if tentatively trying to elicit her help, yet too afraid to directly ask. When she said it had been her first instinct upon receiving my letter to fly out for my surgery, I told her I wanted her there if she felt like she could handle the situation. She wanted to be there, as long as my expectations were reasonable. "You know I don't make chicken soup," she said.

"You know I don't eat chicken," I replied. "I eat Amy's No Chicken Noodle Soup."

"Does that come in a can?"

"Of course," I said.

We booked her a flight for less than three weeks away.

The next day, I slouched onto the couch in my therapist's office and put my water bottle on the table. Shelby adjusted her long peasant skirt, placed a pillow behind her back, and straightened her spine as if to meditate. I grabbed a couch cushion and centered it on my lap. "So," I said, starting to fidget with the cushion's string fringes. "I kind of need one of those therapist's notes. For surgery. I was hoping I wouldn't. It doesn't have to say much. Just that I'm of sound mind to make an adult decision."

"Of course," Shelby said. "My supervisor will have to write it."

Shelby and I had started meeting back when she was in one of those New Age psych grad schools and she was still collecting her clinical hours. In our three and a half years together (with a few breaks), my primary reason for seeing her was the same as the one I had mentioned in my intake interview: dedicating an hour of my week to checking in with myself significantly improved my quality of life.

"I figured your supervisor would have to do it," I said. "But it won't be a problem?"

"Not at all." I could see in her smile that she was glad to help.

I sighed deeply.

"Did you think it would be a problem?" she asked.

I fought the urge to crack a joke about her textbook shrink move. "I just thought your supervisor might have to do a special evaluation or assessment of me."

Shelby shook her head no and it occurred to me that I'd insulted her.

"I know the therapist's note is a technicality," I said. "But I had no idea how nervous I'd feel actually asking for it." I pulled the cushion on my lap closer, hugging it to my stomach. "And every time we talk about surgery, I express some doubts."

"It only makes sense that you have fear and doubts," she said. "If you didn't, then I'd be concerned."

I nodded. Only in my recent conversations with trans guys had I been able to tease out the worries they'd long since forgotten now that they were proud and confident in their bodies and genders.

"I've known you for a long time," Shelby said, "and one thing that I admire about you is the integrity with which you make decisions, your constant striving to know yourself." Without removing my eyes from the mandala behind her, I packed her statement into my affirmation pouch for a rainy day.

The next week she had the letter. I read the few sentences quickly, my eyes honing in on one. "Born female, Nina meets the *DSM-IV* criteria for Gender Identity Disorder." My heart sank. "Really? I thought we were just going to go with the sound mind thing."

She apologized sincerely. "It's the form letter my supervisor uses."

"You do know that diagnosis has the word *stereotypical* in there. Repeatedly," I said. "I don't have some disorder for failing to meet a gender stereotype," I declared, drawing out the last word.

"It's fucked up," she said.

She'd never cursed in my presence before, and it riled me up even more. "I have to live in my body for the rest of my life," I said. "This surgery is a huge gift to myself. I'm spending my entire savings on it, and the fact that I need a piece of paper that says I'm mentally ill really pisses me off."

Shelby kept quiet for a few moments, a move we'd both agreed was helpful when I grew agitated. "You're welcome to write a new letter that she could sign."

I appreciated her offer, but told her to never mind a letter that would yellow in the bottom of some drawer. Only when I left her office with my piece of paper, the key that so many had been forced to acquire by reiterating a standard narrative, the myth of a sole transgender experience that bore no resemblance to mine, did I decide to rewrite the letter, one that I'd make sure would be read.

Dear Dr. Surgeon,

As a small child, Nina Krieger's toys included an entire stable of My Little Ponies as well as a Barbie Glamour Bath and Shower Set. Nina doesn't remember playing with these toys, certainly not aggressively nor in a rough 'n' tumble fashion, but she fondly remembers a picture of herself topless washing her naked Barbie.

Growing up, Nina played many games with her brother and often expressed angst over the one she called the broomstick hoist—she and her friend would loft her brother into the air with a broomstick they'd stuck between his legs. Wondering if Nina's game could be construed as a castration attempt, I hypnotized her to see if perhaps she'd screamed, "You can't have one if I can't have one." But after the hypnosis, she only cried and apologized to her brother.

Nina appears to have had a normal puberty. She responded to menstruation as if she'd sprung a leak, plugging it up like a plumber, and in eighth grade, she showed off her breasts in tight shirts. There appears to have been some adolescent turmoil going on at this time because she brought a carving knife to school and received a suspension. It is impossible to tell if this was a plea for help, but she could've been trying to say, "Look at my tits! Look at my tits, and I'll knife you."

Nina told me she didn't always urinate sitting down and spoke with pride about her ability to aim into a hole in the ground while carrying both her travel backpack and daypack. She also said she didn't care much for toilet paper. "Is that because men don't wipe after peeing?" I asked. "No," she said. "Do you know where toilet paper comes from? Let's save some trees!" I was unable to label her behaviors as cross-gender practices.

As part of my assessment, I sent Nina to a medical doctor who probed for undescended testes below the waist. He also checked her ear canal, nasal pathway, and mouth for gonads passing as tonsils, but found nothing out of the ordinary.

While Nina displayed no diagnosable gender unease throughout childhood, around the age of twenty-six she saw a toddler on a jungle gym wearing a pair of corduroys, Keds, and an Oxford shirt. Shortly thereafter, she began shopping for herself on the boys' side of GapKids.

In conclusion, born female, Nina resembled a girl, then woman, then boy, and is on her way to becoming, well, I have no idea. But whatever the ending, it will be happy. Such is the case when a client writes her own story.

Sincerely,

Dr. Therapist

On the Saturday night before my surgery, I left Sandra and Derek chatting in the corner of the dyke bar that wasn't completely a dyke bar, and waded through the crowd of sporty tomboys in baseball caps, pretty-faced boy-dykes and girl crews that resembled boy bands. I played connect the dots with these images, linking my history into a trajectory that only made sense in hindsight.

I was ordering a glass of water, my taking-it-easy drink, when Greg joined me at the bar. He sported a mustache, a four out of ten on the creepy scale and his only facial hair choice due to his workplace dress code. He ran the back of my fingers along his coarse stubbly cheek. "Impressive," I said, flipping my hand and grazing his other cheek. Greg still pointed out his physical changes at yoga, or when I joined him and Jess at our house to watch football. Two years after his first testosterone shot, and I was invested in his maturation, felt connected to him and his growth by bearing witness to it, and considered him a pretty great guy, even though he'd probably never be one of my best friends.

He clinked his beer against my water. "You ready for Wednesday?" he asked.

"Ready as I'll ever be." I refrained from asking him any anxious questions, since I'd discovered early on that most of his answers involved a dismissive "I don't remember," stifling the conversation and reassurance I sought.

"I'm not sure if Jess told you this already," Greg said, "but I'm trying to start a group. For trans and genderqueer guys." He threw out some new and familiar names.

"Jess mentioned it briefly," I replied.

"It's by invitation only. Kind of a gentlemen's club." Greg dragged his beer closer to himself and circled around his vision of regular get-togethers, support, community. "I see us going away together, a houseboat, a log cabin." He gazed well beyond the shelves of liquor in front of us and shuddered. "Whoa. That just gave me the chills."

I had no interest in grilling meat, driving go-karts, or playing the kind of clubhouse games I envisioned, but I was certainly into the idea of meetings, talks, and sharing. Every trans guy didn't have to be my buddy, but they were all family, and ours was small enough that we had to look out for one another. "Thanks for including me," I said.

"Jess will let you know about our first meeting," he said before heading into the thickening crowd.

I stood alone for a few minutes, thinking back to the first time I'd walked through the doors, how different I was, how different we all must have been when we'd entered this place, before we understood that queers received nine adolescences like cats received nine lives, and the permutations of gender were infinite, the complexities a challenge to explain in a language only built to hold this or that, when many of us were other, something we could see here long before we could speak it.

I looked over at Bec, seated on the covered pool table that had been one of his many stages. Back when I'd just started observing him from afar, I'd watched him perform one of his famous stripteases on that very spot. Lip-synching to the original version of "Fever," he'd run his fingers down the lapels of his gray jacket, flirted with his suspenders, and then tossed a heart-shaped cutout into the crowd before splitting his undershirt down the middle. As he strutted around in his silk boxers, a crowd of mostly dykes went nuts with applause. I imagined they all saw what I did in him, a beauty that transcended gender, only for me this became my guiding light.

Bec and I bumped into each other regularly, but for the most part, I'd maintained my stated position in the corner. Now, on the cusp of a big step on my own path, I wanted to break free from the wall, let him know how much he'd impacted me, just being himself, a seahorse of inspiration. Across the bar, grease held back his neatly combed hair, and underneath his motorcycle jacket, the white of a fresh T-shirt, stretched tightly across his flat chest, glowed. I hesitated for a moment, but my self-conscious fear of going after-school-special cheesy on him fell away as the confidence I'd absorbed from him took over. "Hey," I said, marching directly up to him. "You probably heard," I continued. "I'm having top surgery on Wednesday."

He interrupted my speech with his congratulations.

"Well, I really want to thank you for talking to me about your experience and answering my questions," I said.

Bec flashed his warm, charismatic smile. "I'm happy you made a decision that you believe will increase your comfort." He leaned forward over his crossed legs. "You know what's going to happen?" He grabbed my shoulders and pushed them back. As I opened across the chest, I felt myself extend in every direction. "You're going to grow."

On Tuesday night, after the last yoga class I could attend for six weeks, I picked my mom up at the airport. In the guest bedroom, I showed her all of the printouts I'd made—neighborhood maps, walking routes to gourmet markets with prepared foods, directions to and from the surgery center, everything I'd collected to ease her neurosis and distract me from my own. It was late, after eleven, and lounging on her foam-mattress bed on the floor, we'd somehow fallen into a do-over of the "normal" debate.

I was trying to explain why our family gatherings bothered me—all of the men in matching white button-down shirts debated sports, discussed the economy, and prepared the meat while the women poured the side dishes into bowls from take-out containers, communicated with the hired help, and claimed the seats closest to the kitchen for easy clearing.

"That's the way our family is, same as you are the way you are," my mom said.

"But you all act like your way is the only way, the right way." I wished I could've explained how detrimental gender roles, expectations, and assumptions had been to me, that by not fitting into the system thrust upon me, I'd felt as if there was something inherently wrong with me. I envisioned the somber introductory music of a special with Barbara Walters, the voiceover of her inquisitive rasp: "Tonight, we have cisgender women—girls who wear dresses as children, dresses as teenagers, and dresses as adults—how do they do it? In exclusive interviews, we will meet the family of R., who for safety has requested we use only her first initial." Image cuts to a girl in a dress surrounded by a room full of adults with fuzzed out faces. How would my mom feel if that's how she was represented?

"Honey, my way may not be right, but it's how the world is," she said in the tone a parent reserves to tell a child that life isn't fair.

So put down your seven iron and make change, create a better place for your kid, the old bitter part of me wanted to say. But by flying out to be with me, she'd taken a huge step. And as we set a record for a discussion without escalation, I took my own huge step by appreciating our relationship without complaint. I felt so lucky to have her there in my home that after she held my hand this week, she could ride her golf cart off into the sunset. She'd earned it, passed on to me a life of privilege—there'd been no restrictions on my dreams, even the one to have top surgery. But she'd have to forgive me for leaving my own golf clubs in storage and expanding my interests; having my own needs fulfilled made me want to help those with fewer opportunities and greater challenges, the people who weren't like us.

I slept fitfully that night, with on-and-off thoughts of Bec. As a guest, he'd slept in my room on the eve of his surgery, back before I'd moved in. He'd once told me how he'd tossed and turned, couldn't sleep—he was too excited. He felt like he was going to Disneyland. It was about five in the morning when I woke up for good, wondering if Disneyland would be as magnificent as I imagined it to be.

My mother drove our borrowed car to the surgery center in the touristy Union Square. Within fifteen minutes of arrival, I'd completed all the forms, received my last "good luck" text from Ramona, and left my mom, whom the staff called "The Boss," to wait for me in the prep area. In the privacy of a bathroom, I changed into my gown, compression stockings, booties, and cap. I moved slowly, forcing deep breaths, and carefully placed my clothing in a locker. I would've tossed my Frog Bra in the trash with a "good riddance," if I hadn't known of Big Brother programs, or hadn't acquaintances in great need of pricey binding devices. I washed my face, my locker key bracelet clanking against the sink. On the other wrist, I wore a disposable medical ID. I dried my face with a paper towel and looked into the mirror, holding myself with my eyes. "You can do this, buddy," I said aloud.

Behind a curtain, I sat in a reclining chair, more La-Z-Boy than hospital bed, while a nurse fed me through an IV. My mom remained quiet. She looked like she'd eaten bad sushi, which made me feel like I'd eaten bad sushi. Just as I started to wish my two friends were there to pet my head, coddle, comfort, and warm me with heartfelt words, my mom jumped up. "Excuse me," she said to the nurse, pushing her out of the way with the determination of a New Yorker claiming a rush hour taxi. "I just want to give her a kiss." My mom planted a big wet one on my lips, and a surge of emotions poured out of my eyes.

The nurse handed me a box of tissues just as Brownstein pulled the curtain aside. "Tears already?" he asked.

I wanted to punch him and his infamous bedside manner.

"I hope those are tears of joy," he said.

"Don't worry. All his patients do great," the nurse said to me.

Brownstein offered my mom the opportunity to leave before he marked my chest. I started to nod yes, trying to spare her any extra pain, but my mother shook her head no. While Brownstein undid my gown and drew a dotted line down my sternum, my mother remained with her library book open on her lap. I watched her, jaw clenched, head down, her eyes focused on the page, pretending to read. That's where I got it all, I thought. All of the strength and courage it took to arrive here came from that itty-bitty woman.

When it was time, I walked myself to the operating room, dragging my IV on wheels. I hopped up on the table in the freezing cold room, and before I could be concerned about all of the shiny metallic surfaces and high-tech equipment, the anesthesiologist knocked me out. I opened my eyes to a wall clock that read 12:30 and a nurse asking me to rate my pain on a scale of one to ten with ten being severe. I said two or three. Then I asked for more pain meds. The nurse asked me for another rating. I said one or two. I asked for more meds and she gave them to me. I was floating, breastless and euphoric.

The "congratulations" came in waves, through e-mails, flowers, and cards, including one from my yoga teacher Rusty, which Greg had thoughtfully brought to class for him to sign. Within two days, I weaned myself off the Percocet, because it made me feel emotionally unstable. I was in more discomfort than pain, and it was a consolation to know that the occasional stabbing twinges, like razor blades in my binder, would end. My suffering, the true torture, had come from the constant fight with myself over whether I could, should, or would have this surgery, and had ended the moment my date was finalized.

For the next four days, I melted into the couch, my only goal to rest, not just physically, but also from my thoughts, feelings, and hopes for my new body. Conscious that anything I experienced immediately after surgery was most likely a response to the event itself, I focused only on my DVDs, recuperation, and the distraction from boredom by my visiting friends. Most were meeting my mom for the first time, and watching them help her rotate the plates of gourmet food in the microwave added to my celebration for an event that brought together many of the people closest to me.

By the last day, my mom's surroundings must have sunk in, because she returned home from a walk, sat down in the living room next to a bouquet of tulips and a lone spotted orchid, and asked, "Is *everyone* in the Castro gay?"

"What makes you think people are gay?" I teased.

"I don't know. The hand holding, the couples. I can't be sure. But they are, right?"

"Yes, mom. I was just giving you a hard time."

"I've never been anywhere like it," she said. "It's just different is all."

I was too tired to talk, but I was committed to showing her, someday, that difference was just a matter of perspective. I'd share with her the history of my people, all that I'd discovered in my books, because with an awareness of the past, the legacy of gender variance uncovered, the identities and expressions of me and those around me weren't outlandish or all that different; it was the secrets kept, the stories buried, the trans folk who had to hide their pasts for safety or chose to for other valid, personal reasons that made us seem invisible.

We would have time to talk more now that my mom was with

me in the passenger seat, next to me, by my side. "I'm going to go by a new name," I said, lifting my eyes from my white athletic socks.

I could see the hard outline of my mom's jaw through her cheeks as she clenched her teeth. "Do I need to know it?" Her gaze remained steady, focused on her ankles.

"No, not yet," I said, feeling the relief of my honesty as I spoke.

Like nearly everything I'd given up in the past few years, I held on to "Nina" longer than I might have been comfortable, easing my grip slowly, even as I had learned that letting go of the old was what allowed for new possibilities. A couple weeks ago, my roommates had started to call me "Nick" around the house. It would take some time to get used to this name, develop a relationship with it and make it mine, but hearing "Nick" felt right immediately. I no longer focused on the why, didn't stress about what changing my name would mean in the grand scheme of things, and instead trusted myself, the feeling I now recognized as peace.

As I moved into the unknown, further into the transmasculine realm, I didn't see myself on the path of some big change. But I had less resistance to little changes, to a name that could be screamed in bed, to the male words that made me feel seen, to a chest that others might perceive as being of Man, to fighting my own desires as if for some higher cause, understanding now that I was of most value to myself and to others—women, lesbians, trans guys, lovers, my parents—when I was solid and secure in myself.

The paradox will remain with me forever, the confusing choice to take on a guy's name, even though I do not consider myself a guy. To let words like *Nick*, or even *he* or *she*, create my identity would give too much absolute power to them. I use words to express myself and yet they do not define me, cannot crystallize a life that is in constant flux. Words are tools for communication like gender is a system for organization. And even as I play into the system by choosing a bathroom, a pronoun, a box on a form, I see it as a framework built upon faults, an institution that oppresses us all with some victims suffering more than others, a juggernaut. Some people see it as a binary, a spectrum, a continuum, or a rainbow. But when I envision my own gender, it is with my eye to the lens of a kaleidoscope that I spin and spin and spin.

EPILOGUE

She kissed my stomach gently. I watched her head move up the center of my torso, felt her mouth press into my sensitive skin. "I don't want to hurt you," she said. My chest tingled with pins and needles, a static underneath the surface, raw and alive. Her lips glided along my healing incision, caressing the red, raised line. She pecked the pieces of white gauze still covering my nipples, my surgical pasties. "You're not hurting me," I said.

My chest was tender, my whole upper body sore. That was my own fault, overexerting myself from two days of sex. The Boys had all said the same thing: "Wait, you have the rest of your life to enjoy your new chest. Wait until it heals." But none of them had. What they'd failed to tell me, or what I couldn't understand until now, was that I'd already waited most of my life, certainly my entire relationship with Ramona, for this freedom.

She kissed her way up my center until her breasts lay on the flat table of my chest. She rested her face against mine. I felt the wetness on her cheek, but I did not ask my ex-girlfriend about her tears, same as she hadn't asked me about mine. She was leaving in a few hours for six weeks, enough time for each of us to deal with the consequences of stealing this weekend and reimagining our past.

Ramona nuzzled into my armpit and I nudged her head over, pushing it fully on top of me. "I don't want to hurt you, Nick," she said.

"You're not going to hurt me."

A light rain pebbled the skylight above. Her room was darker than I remembered, even during the day, her bed far from the lone window, facing the mirrored closet. After years of searching my reflection for myself, perhaps I would've found what I wanted had I looked now. Instead, I closed my eyes and felt it, my lover's head resting squarely on my heart.

ACKNOWLEDGMENTS

Thank you, Alex, for your insightful edits, persistent encouragement, and dedication. I am so proud to partner with you. Amy and the other folks at Beacon, thank you for your overwhelming excitement and the opportunity to work with such a remarkable press.

Elizabeth, you were the first person in the industry to believe in this project, and with so much enthusiasm that I thought you had to be nuts. Thank you for being nuts, and for helping me shape my proposal into the foundation for this book.

Lisa, for your vision, friendship, and unwavering belief in me. Jane Anne, for our Friday afternoons. Karl, for being a role model in every way. Stephen, Lewis, Deborah, Aaron and the Lone Mountain crew of my peers, thank you for the truly amazing gift of writing community.

Dad, I hope the overriding sentiment you take away from this book is my love for you. Mom, thank you for supporting my writing despite your complete confusion as to how a creative person emerged from our gene pool. Bro, you are my best friend and that means everything.

I am indebted to many friends for providing feedback on early drafts, keeping me as sane as possible during the later ones, and inspiring me: Derek, Sandra, J. P., Danaa, Meghan, Megann, Liz, Ryan, Molly, Zippy, Breezy, Tom, Dara, Melinda, Brody, Caitlin, Christine, Josie, Solomon, Thea, Betsy, Jody, and my A-gays. Although I am unable to name everyone here, I carry with me every kind and encouraging comment made about my writing.

Janet and Rusty, your love and light are wondrous guides—thank you for breathing with me.

And finally, Kristina, thank you for reading every draft, for your wisdom, and for putting up with me. To be as concise as you have always been: I am so grateful for you.